The
Complete
Book of
MEAT

THE
COMPLETE
BOOK OF
MEAT

by

Phyllis C. Reynolds

M. BARROWS AND COMPANY · NEW YORK

To Samuel Chamberlain for encouraging me to write this book, and to my husband, John, for criticism, praise, and opinions in just the right amounts

Acknowledgments

My sincere thanks are due to Dr. Woodrow J. Aunan, Associate Professor of Animal Husbandry, University of Minnesota, for his guidance, helpful advice and information, and reading of the manuscript; to Mr. Ray Sandin of Hove's Food Market, Inc., for his many Saturday-morning demonstrations in the art of the retail cutting of meat; to the National Live Stock and Meat Board, 36 South Wabash Avenue, Chicago 3, Illinois, for letting me reproduce its photographs and Bone and Cut Charts and for all the information it provided me with on meat; to the American Meat Institute, 59 East Van Buren Street, Chicago 5, Illinois, for letting me quote its instructions for the freezing of meat and for all the information it also provided; and to the many friends who encouraged me to write this book.

P. C. R.

Contents

PART II
HOW MEAT IS CUT
AND HOW TO COOK IT

List of Meat Cuts
and Illustrations

Meat cuts shown in photographs, Bone and Cut Charts, and carving diagrams are listed in **bold** *type. Retail cuts are listed under the names of the wholesale cuts in which they originate.*

BEEF (Continued)

PORK (Continued)

Foreword

In my early days of housekeeping, it was the buying and cooking of meat that provided me with my most harrowing experiences in the kitchen. My husband was a student, the budget was limited, and I had no choice but to learn about cuts of meat other than safe but spendthrift steaks and chops. So, armed with a list of the meats I wanted, or thought I wanted, I went to the supermarket.

I learned early that the labels on the cuts of meat on display were worse than useless for the likes of me. I timed my appearances at the meat counter for moments when no other shoppers were there, pushed the call buzzer to summon the meat cutter, and hoped no one would come by to observe my ignorance as I tried to explain (or find out!) what it was I wanted.

Many were the times I ended up with something I really didn't want because I couldn't answer the meat cutter's questions: How thick do you want it? No, we don't have such-and-such but how about this or that? How much do you want? At home we alternated between meager meals and days of leftovers, absolutely impenetrable pot roast and stew that had fallen to shreds. At dinner, the gaps between courses were unpredictable, as I waited either for the meat or the rest of the dinner to catch up with the other.

I was equipped, of course, with cookbooks. But none of them consistently solved the problem of the right cut of meat for each recipe; sometimes it specified clearly, sometimes it didn't, and if it did specify it never said *why,* let alone described what the cut of meat looked like. At market, on the other hand, looking at the meat wasn't much help when there were, for instance, cuts called "steaks" which I had thought one was supposed to broil but which turned out to be quite impossible for broiling, or "roasts" which I learned to my sorrow could not be roasted.

What I needed was a source to look up two different things: 1) the right cut of meat for a recipe I had already decided on; or 2) the general cooking methods applicable to a cut I had already bought or wanted to buy, so that I could decide on the right recipe.

Economy was my chief concern at first; I learned to braise or stew or "boil" into submission every inexpensive cut of meat there is a name for. But when I overcooked my first filet mignon, I could see I needed insurance against disaster on every level. And when I chose the right piece of meat for a new foreign recipe because I actually could tell from experience what the right one would be (the recipe didn't say what *American* cut to buy), the gleam of authorship began to shine in my eye. I looked at my shelf of cookbooks, some of which had failed me so dismally in the meat department, and determined to learn what they weren't telling me. Many of them were, indeed, very good books. The buying of meat just didn't happen to be their subject.

How to Use This Book

In this book you will find photographs * of practically every
cut of meat available in our markets, accompanied by information on each of the cuts. The various distinguishing muscles
and bones are pointed out in the photographs to help you
further in identifying the cut when you are faced with the real
thing. (Even novice shoppers may not want to go to market
book in hand, though that might not be a bad idea.) With each
cut you will find basic cooking methods provided, or a reference
to such methods to be found in the text or via the Index.

As you can see on the List of Meat Cuts and Illustrations,
p. 9, the retail cuts are discussed under the *wholesale* cuts they
come from. (This is important and the key to the problems you
may be having because of variations in local meat terminology
in your area.) For beef, veal, lamb, and pork you will find a
Cut Chart that diagrams the wholesale cuts and the retail cuts
they contain (the List of Meat Cuts is a summary of these Cut
Charts). And you will find a Bone Chart for each kind of meat;
this is a skeletal diagram of each animal that will also help you
to picture the origin of individual cuts. The text explains to
you where a cut of meat comes from, how tough or tender it may
be, how much bone and fat to expect, and how to cook it. But if
you refer to the Cut and Bone Charts as you read, the logic behind all these explanations will be much clearer to you.

In the description of cuts, I have held mainly to the Chicago

* This collection of photographs was compiled by the National
Live Stock and Meat Board (Chicago, Ill.). They show the retail cuts
as prepared by professional meat cutters in accordance with standard
practice.

style of cutting. For wholesale cuts, the minor variations from the Chicago style that exist across the country do not affect the retail buyer's shopping very much (for beef in particular, see pp. 94-96). But for retail cuts, there are many more regional and local variations, especially in the names used. If you have shopped in several parts of the country, you already know how perplexing this can be.

Nevertheless, with the basic language in this book, you can track down the identity of any unfamiliar cut you come across; and you can ask for a cut you are used to, or a workable approximation of it, even if your name for it isn't the butcher's name for it. This is because both the butcher and this book use the same name for the wholesale cut (and, of course, for many of the retail cuts, too). Use the List of Meat Cuts, or the Bone or Cut Charts, as your point of departure. The retail cut you want, or the one he wants to sell you, must inevitably come from a wholesale cut you can both agree on. It may be necessary, too, to establish what *part* of the wholesale cut the piece of meat in question comes from, but absolute precision isn't necessary. You merely want to know how you should cook the meat and how it will behave when you do. This you can easily find out, once the cut has been located, by referring again to the text.

This book is a shopper's guide to meat and not primarily a cookbook. But it does include over sixty-five special recipes for various cuts of meat and a chapter on sauces for meat. Most important, it also gives instructions for all the basic *methods* of cooking meat. This combination provides a well-rounded repertory of meat cookery all between the covers of one book. The basic methods, however, together with the information on meat itself are intended to take you further afield. With their help you can analyze the recipes in *other* books and know the cuts of meat appropriate for them whenever they do not give adequate guidance themselves. For a quick summary of where the basic cooking methods are discussed, see Chapter 6 and also the Index under the headings of Roasting, Broiling, Panbroiling, Panfrying, Sautéeing, Braising, Stewing, Fricasseeing, and Boiling or Poaching.

Most of these methods—with modifications and plus "Frying" —also apply to chicken. Chickens are called poultry and may sound a little out of place in the context of meat, but they are surely an all-American favorite for the meat course of a good square meal, so there is a chapter on chicken included here, too.

While I was writing this book I was asked questions about meat by people who I had thought were utterly in command of what took place in their kitchens. Not only baffled brides, as I was when I began buying meat, but housewives of some and even long experience are curious about how to use cuts outside the usual list of standbys. Men prove often to be the most interested, and choosy, people in their families when it comes to meat—and they are the ones who ask the questions about carving! Even those who can qualify as "gourmet" cooks will admit that the buying of meat is a major pitfall on the road to creating culinary masterpieces.

Whichever type of cook you may be, this book was written to answer your questions about meat. It should tempt you to use cuts of meat you may not have known what to do with before, and it should add new variety and interest to meals for your family and to festive dinners for your guests. I hope you will enjoy using it as much as I enjoyed writing it.

P. C. R.

PART I

General Information

CHAPTER 1

Where Do You Buy Your Meat?

In the main, you have two choices of where to buy your meat: the self-service counter in a supermarket; or an old-fashioned butcher shop or meat department in a grocery store. Each has its assets and its liabilities and if you are used to shopping in one, shopping in the other can often be a frustrating experience.

For those of you who are happier with the butcher shop, I am sorry to say that supermarket self-service meat departments are apparently here to stay. Every year more and more markets change their meat counters to self-service, which has been found to be both more profitable and more popular with the younger generation.

If you are in a position to make a choice between the two, I hesitate to advise you which to choose. You should perhaps evaluate yourself a little: Are you willing to speak up in the presence of others to say exactly what you want, or, at times, to ask advice or admit ignorance? Are you a precise buyer? Are you an extremely particular buyer? Are you quick at making decisions? Are you willing to pay a little more for a cut if it is exactly what you want? If you are any or all of these, then perhaps you will prefer the butcher shop.

On the other hand, if you like to look over all the available cuts of meat at your leisure before deciding what to have for dinner, or if you do not particularly care for the advice or opinions of a meat cutter, then perhaps you are one for a self-service meat counter.

I must admit that there are times when I am not too happy in a self-service meat department. I find myself wondering what the other side of the meat, which has been so carefully wrapped, looks like. Is the bone bigger or smaller? Is there more or less fat? And that meat cutter who is to be summoned by the buzzer, if I so wish, seems awfully far away. He is just another meat cutter behind the scenes and no one who I could get to know or who would have an inkling of my personal tastes.

However, there are a few things that are important to remember if you choose to do your meat shopping self-service style. First of all, most of the self-service departments do adhere to the cheering line of salesmanship that the customer is always right. If you cannot find a meat cut that pleases you in the display case, you may always request what you want. If you want two pork chops and all you find are packages of three or four, you may ask that a package be divided to get your two. If you are curious about the appearance of the hidden side of a packaged cut, you may ask the attendant to unwrap the package. In fact, you may make use of the self-service department in the same way you would a butcher shop. There is only one problem —although the above practices are not banned in the least, they are not encouraged, for if everyone demanded "special" service, what would be the advantage of a self-service market? So you must have the courage of your convictions.

Whichever type of market you choose, but especially if you choose a butcher shop, it is a good idea to buy as much of your meat as possible at the one store. I don't think I have to elaborate on the advantages of being recognized (and understood) by The Man Behind the Counter.

CHAPTER 2

What Is Meat?

I write this chapter simply because I think you should know what you are biting into when you eat a piece of meat.

Meat is the muscle, and its surrounding connective tissue, of potentially edible animals. As you know, the meat you buy generally contains fat and bone also. Sometimes you think you do not want the latter two, but animals are just made that way, and, unlike the methods used in many foreign countries, American meat-cutting habits call for keeping much of the bone in retail meat cuts. Internal organs, such as kidneys, liver, and sweetbreads (the thymus), are also called meat.

Most of the meat you eat comes from the voluntary muscles, that is, the muscles that move at the animal's will. (The heart, on the other hand, is an involuntary muscle.) Muscles are composed of thousands of muscle fibers; each fiber is a single polynuclear cell; each cell is surrounded by a tender sheath of connective tissue; each small bundle of cells is surrounded by connective tissue; each large bundle of small bundles is surrounded by connective tissue; and each large muscle is even surrounded by connective tissue. So you see—you can't get away from that connective tissue! The bundles of muscle make up the grain of the meat. When the grain is fine, the bundles are small and the connective tissue is thin, and thus the meat is likely to be tender. Tendons in the meat are simply a heavy concentration of connective tissue.

Now that I have the words "connective tissue" firmly implanted in your mind, I shall tell you what it is. It is really not undesirable except in large amounts, for it is the substance which, together with the fat, holds in the meat juices. It is protein, and there are two types: the yellow, elastin, which never becomes tender no matter how long you stew it; and the white, collagen, which softens and changes to gelatin when cooked in water. Therefore, cuts of meat with large amounts of connective tissue have to be cooked by a moist method if they are to be tender.

Whether you like it or not (and you should!), all meat contains fat. Meat containing a good portion of interior fat (marbling) is usually more tender than meat containing little fat. The fat helps to retain juices and consequently the meat does not dry out in cooking. The flavor of the fat joins with that of the lean and increases the over-all flavor of the meat.

Fat is deposited first in the growing animal around the internal organs, such as the kidneys, then around the muscles and under the hide, and last in the muscles themselves (marbling). Thus, an animal has to have a considerable amount of fat elsewhere before his muscles will show any marbling. Young animals have not lived long enough to develop marbling and that is why lamb and veal have little, if any, of it. When the marbling forms, it distends the connective tissue surrounding the muscle fibers, making it thinner and easier to puncture with knife and teeth. The muscles the animals use most—those in the neck, shoulder, legs, and around the joints—have more and thicker connective tissue and less marbling than "supporting" muscles such as the meat in the loin and ribs.

Fat has a lower moisture content than the lean part of meat. Marbling, as it forms, replaces water; and fat in general decreases the water content of the whole animal. The leaner the meat that you buy, the more water you are also buying. This water, if excessive, cooks out when heated.

The lean of meat is largely made up of protein, water, some fatty substances, minerals, and acids. Its color is due to hemoglobin and myoglobin. The older the animal, the more hemoglobin and myoglobin are present in the muscles. Mutton and beef, therefore, are darker in color than young lamb and veal. Pork contains less hemoglobin and myoglobin than do beef and mutton.

The muscles also contain nitrogenous extractives. These extractives are partly responsible for the flavor in meat; and, by acting upon glands in your digestive tract, they stimulate your appetite. Muscles that are used a great deal are richer in extractives than little-used muscles (soup made from beef shank, for instance, is a good beginning for a meal). The older the animal, the more extractives the meat will have, and an animal with a good amount of fat will have more extractives in its muscles than one that has little fat. Pork muscles contain few extractives; the flavoring is in the fat. We can thank Charles Lamb's Bo-bo for discovering that! Unfortunately, nitrogenous extractives are very soluble in water. Cooking by moist heat dissolves much of them and reduces the flavor of the meat. Don't despair, the extractives will all be in the sauce or gravy.

The average American eats more than 160 pounds of meat a year. Research has shown that today cooked meat has 26 per cent fewer calories, 47 per cent less fat, and 23 per cent more protein than cooked meats of yesteryear. Our farmers and ranchers are producing animals that yield more meat, and the packers and processors are trimming fat off meat cuts.

The shift to leaner meat is the result of two main causes. First, it has been found more profitable for farmer, packer, and consumer to increase the more edible portion of meat. Secondly, medical research has been much concerned with the relationship between heart disease and animal-fat consumption. The cholesterol question is still being debated, however. To date there is still no clear indication whether healthy persons who are not decreasing the amount of animal fat in their diets are or are not increasing their chances of acquiring heart disease.

In any case, there is no question that fat left on meat while it is cooking definitely contributes to the flavor of the meat. Avoid eating the cooked fat if you choose, but be prepared to eat less flavorful meat if you remove practically all the fat before you cook the meat.

CHAPTER 3

The Inspection and Grading of Meat

Inspection and grading are two different things, though both are most often done by federal government inspectors.

In the grading of meat there are three determining factors: conformation, finish, and quality. Of course, these factors vary somewhat according to the species of animal being graded. All three are considered in beef and veal grading; in the grading of lamb, yearling lamb, and mutton, two of the factors—conformation and quality—are considered.

Conformation refers to the build of the animal—its shape, contour, the form of the carcass, side, or cut.

Finish refers to the quality, amount, thickness, character, and distribution of the fat. You may have heard your meat cutter speak of a cut as being "well finished"—that doesn't mean the meat has been highly polished!

Quality refers to certain characteristics of the lean, fat, tissue, and bone. The color and texture of the meat, the extent of marbling, the firmness and strength of the muscle fibers and connective tissue, and the size and strength of the bone are all considered.

I shall discuss further what you should look for in the meat you buy in the separate chapters on each kind of meat in Part II.

For many years now most of the meat you have bought has been federally inspected, although meat from locally slaughtered animals that is to be sold within the state may be inspected by the local city or state government. Inspection assures you that the meat is wholesome and free from disease when it leaves the packing house. The purple circle around the legend "U.S. INSP'D & P'S'D" stamped on the fat signifies that the meat has passed federal inspection standards.

Most of the meat you buy has also been federally graded. However, many packers have their own grades, which they indicate with brand names and which, in general, closely parallel those of the government. It is wise to learn what these packers' brand names signify; this will help you in buying meat that has perhaps not been federally graded.

The men who grade meat have been highly trained for their job. The purpose of federal grading is to assure you that the meat you buy will be of a certain quality. Federal grading is handled by the Department of Agriculture, and the standards set up for meat found in retail markets are listed as:

Prime (beef, veal, and lamb); **Choice** (beef, veal, and lamb); **Good** (beef, veal, and lamb); **Standard** (beef and veal); **Commercial** (beef); and **Utility** (beef, veal, and lamb). The grades are stamped, again in purple, on the full length of the carcass; the grade and the letters "U S D A" are enclosed in a shield. (The grade of the meat you buy prepackaged in supermarkets usually is printed on the price tag of each package.)

Pork is generally not federally graded; it is, however, federally inspected. It is graded by the packer, who uses his own brand names to designate grades.

I shall briefly describe here the grades of beef and lamb. The grading of veal, yearling mutton, and mutton is similar. But veal comes from a young animal (vealer or calf) and mutton from an older sheep; consequently there will be some difference, especially in the amount of fat—less in veal than in beef, more in mutton than in lamb. It will be to your advantage to learn to recognize in retail cuts the characteristics described below, for there is some variation within the grade as well as from grade to grade.

⚘ **BEEF—Steers, Heifers, and Cows—Minimum qualifications for each grade:**
(See Beef Cut Chart, p. 95, for the location of wholesale cuts mentioned below; see standing rib, p. 117, for clear identification of the rib "eye" muscle.)

Prime (cow beef is not eligible for Prime): The carcasses and wholesale cuts are blocky, compact, and very thickly fleshed. The fat covering is fairly smooth and uniformly distributed over the exterior surface. Feathering (the intermingling of fat and lean between the ribs, which to me resembles half of a herringbone design) is generous. The interior and exterior fats are firm, brittle, and somewhat waxy. The cut surface of the rib "eye" muscle is firm with a smooth velvety appearance; it has extensive, abundant marbling, and its color is uniform and bright and may range from pale red to a deep blood red.*

Prime beef constitutes a very small percentage of all marketed beef. Many meat markets consider it to be excessively fat for good retail selling and most of it is bought by "better" restaurants and hotels, as they have obvious methods of absorbing the expense of weight that includes excess fat.

Choice: The carcasses and wholesale cuts are moderately blocky, compact, and thick fleshed. The fat covering varies within moderate limits depending upon the maturity of the animal. Interior and exterior fats are fairly firm and brittle and there is a moderate amount of feathering. The cut surface of the rib "eye" varies according to the maturity of the animal. In younger animals it has a moderate amount of marbling and it is usually slightly soft but fine in texture; in the older animals it has fairly abundant marbling and it is moderately firm and fine in texture. Its color ranges from light red to slightly dark red and is generally uniform and bright.

Choice meat is your best buy, a good combination of palatability and reasonable cost. Most retail markets consistently carry Choice meat, and it is usually their biggest seller.

* Red meat is almost purple when it is first cut and acquires its familiar red color after it is exposed to air.

Good: The carcasses and wholesale cuts are slightly compact and blocky in conformation and they are slightly thick fleshed. The fat covering varies, depending on the maturity of the animal, being thin over the loins and ribs and over the portions of the rounds and chucks in the younger animal, and slightly thick and extending over most of the round and chuck in the older animal. The younger animal has a small quantity of feathering and the older animal has moderately abundant feathering. The fat may be somewhat soft or slightly oily. The cut surface of the rib "eye" varies according to the maturity of the animal. It may have a slight amount of marbling and is usually moderately soft but fine in texture in the younger animal. There may be a modest amount of marbling, and the muscle is usually slightly soft but moderately fine in texture in the more mature animal. The color of the muscle varies from a light red to a slightly dark red.

Many meat markets offer Good meat for the "penny-wise consumer."

Standard: This is a comparatively new grade for beef. In June, 1956, the Commercial grade was divided into Standard for young animals and Commercial for mature animals.

The carcasses and wholesale cuts of the Standard grade are rangy, angular, and slightly thin fleshed. The fat covering varies from thin over the loin and ribs in the younger animals to slightly thin over the loin and ribs, and it partially covers the outside of the rounds and chucks in the older animals. The young animals will have very scanty feathering between the ribs, while the older animals will have a small amount. The fat is moderately soft. The rib "eye" varies from moderately soft, moderately fine in texture, with a slight amount of marbling in the older animals, to somewhat soft and watery but fine in texture and with practically no marbling in the younger animals. The color of the lean varies from light red to a slightly dark red.

Some markets carry this grade of meat for customers who want a high porportion of lean to fat. It is sometimes called "economy beef." The market will usually tell you that this grade is not as tender or as flavorful as the higher grades (due in part to the lack of fat and the young age of the animal).

It is most unlikely that you will ever see either of the two following grades in your market, but their description gives you a good idea of what you do *not* want in meat!

Commercial: The carcasses and wholesale cuts are slightly thick fleshed but rather irregular and rough in contour. The amount of fat varies, depending on the maturity of the animal; however, the fat is firm. In carcasses which only slightly exceed the minimum maturity permitted, the cut surface of the rib "eye" is moderately firm and slightly coarse in texture and will have a moderate amount of marbling. In older animals the rib "eye" is firm but coarse in texture and the marbling will be moderately abundant but also rather coarse and prominent. The lean color varies from slightly dark red to dark red in color.

Utility: The carcasses and wholesale cuts may be decidedly rangy, angular, and irregular in conformation. The fleshing is usually thin. The degree of fat covering varies according to the maturity of the animal. The quantity of interior fat varies from very little to a moderate amount. The fat is usually soft. The cut surface of the lean muscle is usually soft and watery in the younger animal and in the older animal it is usually fairly firm but coarse. There is practically no marbling except in the meat from older animals. The color ranges from a light red to a very dark red.

❀ LAMB—Minimum qualifications for each grade:

(See Lamb Cut Chart, p. 198, for location of wholesale cuts mentioned below.)

Prime: Carcasses are compact and blocky and tend to have plump, full legs; wide, thick backs; thick, full, smooth shoulders. Quality varies with maturity. Young lambs have red, narrow rib bones and a moderate amount of feathering. The inside of the flank is light pink and the exterior finish is firm. More mature lambs have somewhat wider, slightly red rib bones and there is rather extensive feathering. The inside of the flank is dark pink. The external finish is very firm.

Choice: Carcasses are slightly compact with slightly plump, full legs; slightly wide, thick backs; slightly wide, full shoulders. Quality varies with maturity. Young lambs have red, narrow rib bones and a small amount of feathering. The inside of the flank is a darker pink. The exterior finish is moderately firm. More mature lambs have somewhat wider, slightly red rib bones, and a moderate amount of feathering. The inside of the flank is light red. The external finish is firm.

Good: Carcasses are moderately rangy and slightly angular with slightly thin, tapering legs; slightly narrow, thin backs and shoulders. Quality varies with maturity. Young lambs have red, narrow rib bones and traces of feathering. The inside of the flank is dark pink and the exterior finish is somewhat firm. More mature lambs have somewhat wider, slightly red rib bones and a slight amount of feathering. The inside of the flank is darker red and the external finish is moderately firm.

Utility: Carcasses are very rangy and angular with thin, slightly concave legs; very narrow, sunken backs; narrow, sharp shoulders. There is practically no feathering. The lean of the inside flank muscle and that between the ribs is dark red. The external finish is soft.

CHAPTER 4

The Storage and Freezing of Meat

IN THE REFRIGERATOR

Fresh meat should be put in the fresh-food or meat compartment of your refrigerator as soon as possible after it arrives from the market. If the meat has been wrapped in market (butcher) paper, unwrap it, as the paper will probably stick to the meat. Put it in a dish or plate, and cover it tightly so that it will not absorb refrigerator odors. If the meat has lost its chill en route from market to refrigerator, put it in a dish or plate and cover it loosely with waxed paper. Keep it thus, in the refrigerator, for about an hour or until it has again become cold; then cover it tightly. Most prepackaged meat that you buy in a self-service meat department may be left in its original wrapper if it is to be used within two or three days. The film wrapping used does not stick to the meat and has been especially treated to slow down the entrance of air and the escape of moisture.

Meat such as steaks, chops, and roasts should be cooked within three to four days of purchase. If you plan to hold them longer, wrap them properly and keep them in your frozen-food compartment for a period of up to a week. Ground meat is more perishable and should be cooked within a day of purchase. Keep it in the frozen-food compartment if you want to hold it longer. Liver, kidneys, heart, brains, and sweetbreads are also very perishable. Plan your shopping so you can cook and eat these cuts the same day that you buy them. They may be stored in the frozen-food compartment, but freezing and thawing such cuts seem to take much of the juice out of them. Even if they have been wrapped in film at the supermarket, these meats, and ground meat, should be unwrapped and stored in a covered dish.

Fresh meat should be kept for a period of only one week, preferably less, at freezing temperatures above 0°F. The temperature of the ice-cube section of a refrigerator, and often of its frozen-food compartment, is well above 0°F. (It is generally around 10° to 15°F.) There is a definite decrease in quality and vitamin content if the meat is kept for a period longer than a week. And temperatures above 0°F. do not restrict undesirable enzyme action, which results in unpleasant flavors and changes in color.

If you do intend to keep a cut of meat in your frozen-food compartment, unwrap it (if it has been wrapped in market paper) as soon as possible and rewrap it in special freezer paper. You may, however, let your meat remain in the original package if it has been purchased from a self-service meat department and you are sure there are no breaks in the wrapping. Chops, steak, or ground-meat patties should be separated by two pieces of freezer paper before being wrapped into a larger package.

All meats kept in your frozen-food compartment may be thawed in the refrigerator, which takes several hours (12 to 24); or at room temperature, which takes a few hours; or at room temperature in front of an electric fan, which hastens thawing. Never thaw meat in water, for you will lose the valuable juices that are released during the thawing process.

Thin cuts of meat, such as steaks or chops, may be cooked unthawed or partially thawed. If the meat is to be dredged with flour or if it is to be breaded, it should be at least partially thawed. Even a roast may be cooked unthawed. Remember, however, that this lengthens the cooking time and that you will not be able to insert a meat thermometer at the beginning of the cooking.

Cured meat, such as ham or bacon, and precooked meat, such as cold cuts or frankfurters, should not be kept in the frozen-food compartment. The presence of salt in such meats interferes with proper freezing of the fat. The texture of hot dogs or frankfurters and similar meats changes upon freezing. Keep all these meats in the fresh-food compartment and do not store them much longer than a week—two weeks at the most. They may remain in their original wrapping unless it is market paper.

Cooked meat and leftover meat that you plan to store in the refrigerator should be cooled as fast as possible. It should then be covered and kept in the refrigerator.

The distinction between keeping meat in the frozen-food compartment of a refrigerator and in a freezer must be stressed. Effective, long-term (over a week) freezing *cannot* be done in the frozen-food compartment when the temperature is above 0°F.

IN THE FREEZER

Many refrigerators today do have freezer compartments that will maintain 0°F. This is the *highest* temperature that should be used for the storage of meat for a period longer than a week. Home freezers and commercial locker plants maintain a temperature of 0°F. or lower. Storage of meat at this low temperature causes almost complete inactivity of enzymes and of most bacteria.

Lean meat is composed of from 60 to 65 per cent water. The slow freezing of meat—either in your refrigerator at 0°F. or above, or in a freezer at just 0°F.—causes the water to separate from the rest of the cell contents. It collects and forms large crystals. These crystals stretch and rupture the cell walls in only a few places. When meat is frozen quickly (flash-freezing) and at a sub-zero temperature (usually −35°F. or below), there is very little separation of the water from the rest of the cell. Tiny crystals—many in the place of one large one—are formed. These crystals rupture the cell walls and connective tissues in many places. Thus, the rapid freezing of meat at a sub-zero temperature and storage for several weeks or longer at 0°F. actually tenderize the meat to a certain extent.

However, don't run to the store and buy a Utility grade porterhouse steak, freeze it at −35°F., and expect to bite into a Prime grade porterhouse after you cook it! On the other hand, it has been found that meat, especially beef, of a *high grade,* after being quickly frozen at a sub-zero temperature and then held at 0°F. for about six months, will be just as tender as if it had been aged about two weeks.

Prolonged aging of beef and lamb before freezing shortens the period of time the meat can be stored. The longer the meat is aged, the more oxygen the fat absorbs; this will cause the frozen fat to become rancid more quickly. The hindquarter of good quality beef may be aged for about ten days and the forequarter for about six days. Beef of lower quality should not be aged over five days. Lamb and mutton may be aged for about five to six days. If the aging period has been longer than that recommended, the fat that has been exposed to air should be cut off. (See Chapter 5 for more about the process of aging.)

If you store your foods in a commercial locker, your locker operator can advise you about your meat storage. When you purchase a refrigerator with a zero freezer or when you purchase a home freezer, you will receive instructions from the manufacturer on the freezing and storage of meat. If you should not have such instructions, use the following guide prepared by the American Meat Institute:

STORAGE OF MEAT IN THE HOME FREEZER *

ॐ How to Prepare Meat for Freezing

Refrigerate meat promptly after purchase. The meat has been kept under refrigeration constantly in the supermarket to preserve its goodness and it deserves the same kind of treatment in your home.

If you plan to freeze the meat, do it as soon as possible. The fresher the meat, the better its keeping quality will be while frozen. Remember, freezing doesn't improve meat; it can only keep the meat as good as it was before freezing.

Wrap meat in meal-size portions, planning on guest meals as well as family meals. Rotate frozen meats so you use first the food which has been stored longest.

Before freezing, have the meat ready for cooking—prepared, shaped, and trimmed just as you want to cook it. For stews, bone and cube before freezing. For beef loaves and patties, grind

* Courtesy the American Meat Institute, 59 East Van Buren Street, Chicago 5, Illinois.

meat before freezing. Season meat, if you like, with salt and pepper and/or other dry seasonings.

⚙ How to Wrap Meat for Freezing

For short periods in the freezer (no longer than one to two weeks), prepackaged self-service meats may be frozen in the original store package (film and board or tray). Make sure, though, that there are no breaks in the package.

For longer periods in the freezer, use special freezer wrapping materials. Either of the following methods of wrapping is recommended:

A single moisture-vapor-proof sheet or bag which may be tied, taped, heat-sealed, or folded. This single sheet should be strong enough to resist puncturing and tearing.

Or a double wrap consisting of:

a. An inner wrap of moisture-vapor-proof paper, cellophane, pliofilm, aluminum foil, or other special freezer-storage types of packaging materials available on the market. (Ordinary waxed paper is not moisture-vapor-proof and therefore is not satisfactory.)

b. An outer wrap of special packaging material or heavy wrapping paper. If an outer wrap of high heat-insulating value is used (several thicknesses of wrapping paper, for example), the meat should be inner wrapped and frozen before the outer wrap is applied.

Meats wrapped in ordinary market paper should be unwrapped and then rewrapped for freezing as outlined here.

A satisfactory method of making a package for freezing is as follows:

1. Use enough paper so the edges may be folded down at least three times.

2. Place the meat in the center of the paper.

3. Separate individual servings (such as steaks, chops, or ground-meat patties) with sheets of freezer paper so they will come apart easily before cooking.

4. Bring two edges of paper together above the meat and fold down in ½-inch to 1-inch folds until the paper is tight against the meat.

5. Press the wrap closely to the meat to force out air.

6. Seal edges carefully with freezer tape, or fold over ends at least twice and tie securely.

Mark each frozen meat package to show contents, number of servings, and date of freezing.

❀ How to Freeze Meat

Freeze meats promptly at 0°F. or lower. If your refrigerator or freezer is not capable of maintaining a temperature of 0°F., do not attempt to freeze meat in it. To check the temperature of your refrigerator or freezer, use a thermometer manufactured for this purpose. If your refrigerator or freezer has a temperature control knob, adjust it as necessary to obtain 0°F. or lower. Do not freeze too many packages at a time, so that uniformly low temperatures will be maintained. Follow freezing directions in instruction book which accompanied freezer or refrigerator.

❀ How to Store Frozen Meat

Frozen meat should be stored in a freezer or in the freezer section of a refrigerator where a temperature of 0°F. or lower can be maintained. The frozen-food storage compartment or ice-cube section of the refrigerator, if it does not maintain temperatures of 0°F. or lower, is not recommended for keeping frozen meat longer than a week. To maintain its flavor, color, texture, and appearance, meat should be stored *no longer* than the periods shown in the following table:

Product	Recommended Maximum Storage Time at 0°F. or Lower
Beef	6-8 months
Fresh Pork and Veal	3-4 months
Lamb	6-7 months
Ground Beef	3-4 months
Variety Meats (Liver, Heart, Tongue, etc.)	3-4 months
Smoked Hams, Picnics, and Slab Bacon (Whole, Halves, or Quarters)	Not to exceed 60 days
Other Cured and Smoked Meats	Not to exceed 60 days
Sliced Bacon	Not recommended for freezing
Bologna, Frankfurters, or Weiners	Not recommended for freezing
Fresh Pork Sausage	Not recommended for freezing
Poultry *	
Giblets	4 months
Chicken	6-12 months
Turkey	6-12 months

Cured and smoked meats and fresh pork sausage deteriorate rapidly in flavor when frozen. Thus, it is recommended that some of these products not be frozen and that others be stored

* Information supplied by the Home Economics Department of the Poultry & Egg National Board, St. Charles, Illinois.

frozen for only limited periods. Perishable canned hams (3 pounds or over) should not be frozen; they should be stored at refrigerator temperatures (30 to 40°F.) in the unopened can until used.

For maximum use of freezer and for best storage of meats in the freezer, consult your refrigerator or freezer instruction book.

⊛ How to Prepare Frozen Meat for Cooking

Frozen prepared meat dishes, such as meats in combination with other foods and meat pies, should be cooked from the frozen state. Other meats may be cooked while hard-frozen, except those meats that need shaping or breading before cooking.

Thaw frozen meats, without unwrapping, in the refrigerator. In general, refrigerator thawing of meats requires 5 to 8 hours per pound, but the time will vary depending on size, shape, and thickness of meat. Thawing of meats at room temperature is not recommended since meat will spoil readily if allowed to stand too long at such temperatures. If necessary to hasten thawing, place wrapped frozen meats in cold running water. Allow 2 to 6 hours. If the meat was frozen in the store package on a board or tray, thaw partially to make it easier to remove board or tray. Otherwise, pieces of the board may stick to the meat. Never immerse unwrapped meat in water for thawing, unless it is to be cooked in the water as are stews.

All meat should be cooked as soon as it is completely thawed. Once meat has thawed completely, it should not be refrozen because juices are lost during thawing and because the meat may deteriorate between the time of thawing and refreezing. If meat has thawed partially and still shows ice crystals, refreezing is possible, but not advisable. After cooking, the meat may be frozen.

⚙ How to Cook Frozen Meats

Roasting: Hard-frozen oven roasts require approximately one-third to one-half again as much cooking time per pound as do the corresponding fresh roasts.* Some branded frozen roasts are preweighed and carry cooking instructions from the frozen or thawed state. Without such instructions, use the same procedures for roasting hard-frozen meat as for fresh or completely thawed roasts; place meat on a rack, roast in a 325°F. oven. Do not cover pan, do not add water, and do not baste during cooking. Use a meat thermometer to determine the doneness of the meat, and insert it in the roast after the center of the meat is thawed or when it is about half-done. (Do not force thermometer into partially thawed meat; it may break if the roast is still hard-frozen in center.)

Broiling: Thin-cut hard-frozen steaks require very little more broiling time than the same cuts of fresh meat.† Thicker cuts of hard-frozen steaks will require one-quarter more to two times as much broiling time as the corresponding fresh cuts. Because frozen steaks need slower cooking, place the hard-frozen steaks at least four inches below source of heat so the exterior surface does not overcook before the interior is done. If impossible to lower the broiling rack, reduce broiling temperature. Follow the same broiling procedures as with fresh or thawed meats. [See Chapter 6.]

Panbroiling: Hard-frozen thin steaks and chops require very little more panbroiling time than do the same cuts of fresh meats. Allow one-quarter to one-half again as much time for

* See Roasting Times and Temperatures in the Appendix.
† See Broiling Times and Temperatures in the Appendix.

thicker cuts of hard-frozen meats as recommended for the corresponding fresh cuts. To panbroil hard-frozen thin cuts, dust lightly with a little flour, then heat a heavy skillet, add about a tablespoon of fat, and brown meat quickly on both sides. Hard-frozen thicker cuts need not be dusted with flour, but after browning in a lightly greased hot skillet, the heat should be lowered so that the meat cooks without excess browning.

Braising: Frozen meats to be braised take little or no longer than the corresponding cuts of fresh meat. If meat is to be floured before browning and cooking in water, as pot roasts, for example, thaw meat slightly, and dredge with, or pound in, flour. Meats that require no flouring may be browned without thawing, but require a little additional cooking time. Follow the same braising procedure as for fresh meat. [See Chapter 6.]

Cooking in Water: Frozen meats to be cooked in water take little or no longer than corresponding fresh cuts. The longer cooking times are required for larger pieces of frozen meat. Prepare frozen meat for cooking in water as the fresh cuts are prepared. [See Chapter 6.]

CHAPTER 5

The Aging of Meat

Some people enjoy the flavor of well-aged meat, and in my opinion aging does improve flavor. Only beef and sometimes lamb and mutton are aged. But these meats are aged only if they are from a high-grade carcass. In other words, to be eligible for aging, the meat must have a uniform covering of sufficiently thick fat. This covering of fat inhibits the penetration of oxygen to the lean, thus preventing bacterial action, discoloration, and evaporation.

Aging also tenderizes high-grade beef, mutton, and lamb. Absolutely fresh meat is always rather tough. It is only after the initial one to two days of hanging (under refrigeration) at the packing house that meat begins to become tender. During the aging process the small amount of sugar present in the muscles changes to lactic acid. This acid attacks the tough connective tissues, reducing them to a partially gelatinous state.

The period of aging ranges from two to six weeks. The tenderizing (enzymatic) process usually slows down after about twenty-one days and is gradually replaced, starting on the exterior fat, by bacterial decomposition. The person who enjoys a "high" flavor likes his meat aged four weeks or more. After six weeks of aging the decomposition process has entered the interior lean to such an extent that the meat is no longer palatable to most people.

The aging process is carried out at a temperature ranging from 36° to 42°F. with a relative humidity of from 75 to 85 per cent to keep the meat from drying out. Sometimes the packing plant will age the meat purchased by a particular market, and sometimes the retail market, or restaurant, or other wholesale purchaser, will do its own aging. If you are interested in buying aged meat, ask your butcher if his meat is aged and for how long a period. Some markets that age meat for ten days or less will gladly age it longer for you upon specific request.

Veal is not aged because it lacks sufficient fat. The aging process does not improve pork.

A new method for tenderizing meat is presently being instituted by some packing houses that may in large part supplant aging. For many years it has been known that enzymes of plant origin—especially from papayas, pineapple, lemon (see Basic Marinade, Chapter 7)—are effective meat-tenderizing agents. After much study and experimentation, a technique was devised whereby the animal is injected with the enzyme "papayan" ten to thirty minutes before it is slaughtered. After the animal is slaughtered, the muscle temperature drops, inhibiting enzyme action. Subsequent refrigeration also inhibits enzyme activity, and it is only when the retail meat cut is cooked—and then only during the interval that the cooking temperature is within the range of 120° to 160°F.—that the enzyme is active. After the temperature has reached 160°F. the enzyme is destroyed by the heat, and the "aging" process (at least the tenderizing aspect of it) has in essence taken place during the cooking of the meat.

This method will result in a much greater yield of meat that may successfully be roasted, rather than cooked by methods such as braising or pot-roasting that are recommended for tougher cuts—chuck roast, for instance. And, of course, it will also be used on animals of lower grades, thus increasing the supply of edible meat.

CHAPTER 6

The Various Methods
of Cooking Meat

Why cook meat? That's a silly question! "Because it tastes better cooked," you answer. Okay, why does it taste better? Because the collagen is often converted to gelatin, some of the adipose tissue is melted, and the albumin and globulin are coagulated—and civilized human beings seem to like it better that way. In other words, the cooking of meat usually makes it more attractive, more tender, and more flavorful. Also—for the hygiene-minded—meat is cooked to destroy any possibly harmful germs.

There are really only two methods of cooking meat: by dry heat and by moist heat. Generally, dry heat does not increase tenderness and it may even reduce it. Moist heat increases tenderness by softening the connective tissue (collagen) and turning it to gelatin. Tender cuts of meat, such as those from the loin and ribs—the supporting muscles that contain little connective tissue—are most often cooked by dry heat. The less tender cuts—the more greatly exercised muscles that contain large amounts of connective tissue—are more often cooked by moist heat.

The methods of dry heat are: roasting, broiling, panbroiling, and frying. The methods of moist heat are: braising, stewing, fricasseeing, and poaching (simmering or "cooking in water"). Sautéing comes under either heading, according to the elaborations there may be in the recipe used.

A few cuts which should qualify for the dry-heat method but usually are cooked by moist heat: chops, steaks, and cutlets of pork and veal. These meats should be cooked to a well-done stage. Braising or sautéing them (on top of the stove) cooks them to well-done without drying them out.

❀ How Much Meat per Person?

This has to be decided before you cook it. Perhaps the safest way to gauge the amount of meat to buy is to use the popular rule of thumb: ¼ pound of meat per person if there is little fat and no bone; ⅓ pound per person if there is some fat and a small amount of bone; ½ to ¾ pound per person if there is an ample amount of fat and bone; and 1 pound per person if there is little lean. It is almost impossible to say exactly how much of a particular cut you should buy, for meat markets do vary in how they prepare cuts for retail sale.

Of course, you should always take the following into account. Are you feeding, for instance, four hale and hearty men or four watching-their-figures women? Are you serving the meal indoors or outdoors (that fresh air always does it!)? Are you serving several courses or just one main course? Are you serving the meat with garnishes such as mushrooms, vegetables, etc.? Are you serving the meat with or without a rich sauce?

Look at the relevant Bone Chart (Beef, Veal, Lamb, or Pork) before you buy a roast in order to get an idea of how much hidden bone you will be getting, and remember that such meats as spareribs, chicken, oxtail contain a great deal of bone.

Packing houses more and more often, now, are removing excess bone and fat from meat. This trend is making it much easier to know the amount of lean you are buying and much more convenient to cook and carve certain cuts. Uncanned ham was one of the first cuts of meat to be handled in this way. It is a delight.

NINE BASIC METHODS OF COOKING MEAT

✿ To Roast

Only tender meat can be cooked in this way. The meat is placed, fat side up, on a rack (unless the cut is a rib roast—the ribs then form their own rack) in a pan and cooked, uncovered, in the oven. No liquid is added. The original method of roasting, and one that has made a comeback in popularity, is that of putting the meat on a spit and cooking it over an open fire or barbecue grill, or in an electric rotisserie.

To prepare meat for roasting one may salt and pepper it; rub pepper and herbs into the fat; lard it if it is lean, seasoning the lardoons; insert slivers of garlic into it at intervals (make cut with small knife, push knife away from you while it is still in the meat—broad side facing you—insert piece of garlic, and remove knife). Most of the salt added before roasting runs down the sides of the meat with the melting fat. A greater quantity of salt can be absorbed if it is added bit by bit throughout the roasting period, although it has been found that salt penetrates only about half an inch into the meat in any case.

The temperature at which the oven should be set varies according to the type of meat to be roasted. The temperatures are given in the chapters on specific types of meat and, for convenience sake, they are set up in chart form in the Appendix to this book. The length of cooking time varies also. You will find this information in the later chapters. The use of a meat thermometer is the surest way of cooking your roast to the desired doneness.

Many cooks still advocate the searing of roasts. It is maintained that this method makes a better looking and more palatable roast. The meat is put in a 500° oven until it is well browned (about 20 minutes). The heat is then reduced to about 300° and the roast is cooked until done. It was once thought that this method sealed in the juices; however, just the opposite has been found to be true—in the long run a much greater amount of juice is lost by searing.

The conventional method of roasting today calls for a constant oven temperature between 300° and 350°. If a browner roast is desired, the temperature may be raised to 450° or 500° for the last five to ten minutes of the roasting period. Searing at this point does not seem to cause an excessive loss of juices.

There is yet another method of roasting beef and lamb which has rightly been gaining in popularity. It can be called the "all-day" method, and it provides numerous advantages to anyone equipped with time and a meat thermometer. As is suggested above, research has shown that the lower the roasting temperature, the less meat juice is lost. This finding has resulted in the all-day method, which calls for an oven temperature of 200°, or even a little less if possible. The end product is a much more uniformly cooked roast (and what an advantage this is if you are serving several persons who like the same degree of doneness) that has lost practically none of its liquid to the roasting pan.

The only difference in prescribing the all-day method is that variations inherent in roasts do not permit cooking times to be precisely established. A good rule of thumb is that this method

usually takes double the conventional (300°-350°) times, but the
meat thermometer is still essential. If the roast seems to be ap-
proaching the desired end temperature too early, you need only
remove the roast from the oven for a short time. Fifteen minutes
or so out of the oven will effectively slow the cooking process.
You may remove the roast two or three times like this if necessary. The end searing, as in conventional roasting, can also be
done with the all-day method.

No matter how you roast your meat, if it is removed from the
oven about fifteen minutes before the end of the cooking time
(it will continue to cook by itself), the carving will be easier
because the collagen will have an opportunity to set.

❀ To Broil

Only tender meat can be cooked this way. The cooking is
done by direct heat in the broiling unit of the stove or over
coals in your barbecue.

As in roasting, there is more than one school of thought on
broiling. Some advocate a constant high heat (unless the meat
is over 2½ inches thick) and others advocate a steady moderate
(350°) heat. The latter school allows a preliminary searing at
times. I cannot say that one method is better than the other.
You should try both to see which pleases you. A high heat or
preliminary searing will smoke up your kitchen more, and
there is a chance of flames and of burning the exterior of the
meat or the bones. But moderate heat seems to give less color
to the exterior and you run a greater risk of cooking the meat
past the degree of rareness you want. Perhaps one good rule to
follow is: The thicker the meat, the more reason to sear, then
broil at a moderate temperature; if you are not indulging in a
lavish steak, simply broil at a moderate temperature.

Some electric stoves have a "broil" setting on the oven gauge; some older gas stoves leave you to judge the correct heat by the size of the flame only. If you are successful with meat over an outdoor barbecue, where you rely solely on sight, broiling meat in your stove should be no more of a problem.

The broiler should be preheated and the rack may be rubbed with fat to prevent initial sticking. The exterior fat of the meat should be scored (cut at right angles to the muscle, being careful not to cut the muscle itself) at intervals to prevent curling. Some cooks say to place the meat three inches from the flame; others give you a leeway of up to five inches. The distance you use will vary the length of cooking time and may determine the ultimate appearance of the steak. I believe three inches is generally the best distance to use. While the meat is broiling it may be brushed occasionally with butter or oil to prevent the outside from drying out. Turn your meat with pincers—don't pierce it with a fork, for the valuable juices will spurt out.

You may season the meat before turning it and again at the end of the cooking time, or you may apply all the seasoning just before serving.

The length of broiling time varies for the type of cut and the size. In later chapters I shall give you times, and these are also charted in the Appendix to this book, but they will be only approximate. There are four ways of telling when the meat is done: 1) By the use of a meat thermometer, which should be inserted into the middle of the edge of the meat (use the same temperature guide as you would for a roast). Be sure that the thermometer is secure in the meat; this is only possible if the cut is over $1\frac{1}{2}$ inches thick. If you are broiling with gas, be careful not to let the thermometer come in contact with the flame. 2) By touch. When pressed, the exterior of the meat will be resistant. 3) By the appearance of drops of red liquid on the surface of the meat (this is the juice from the center coming to the surface). Naturally, if you do not like any degree of rareness, you should wait until the red drops have disappeared. 4) By a small cut made with a knife near the bone (of course, you will lose some juice). If you have any doubts, this last method is perhaps the surest.

✿ To Panbroil

Again, only tender meat can be used for this type of cooking. The meat is grilled in a thick, ungreased skillet, or the skillet may be rubbed with a small amount of fat at the beginning to prevent sticking. A light sprinkling of salt in the skillet also prevents initial sticking. The skillet should be hot (but not smoking!) when you put in the meat. The length of cooking time in panbroiling is somewhat less than in broiling. The variations in degree of heat are the same as in broiling.

✿ To Panfry

Meat that can be broiled can also be panfried in a skillet. This is different from panbroiling in that fat is used for the frying, somewhat more fat, even, than in sautéing (see below). Meat to be panfried is generally dredged with seasoned flour, or breaded, and then browned in the fat. The skillet usually should not be covered. The meat is cooked at a moderate temperature and is turned occasionally to cook both sides evenly.

✿ To Sauté

The word sauté comes from the French verb *sauter,* which means to jump, leap, or skip. Literally, to sauté means to cook meat over a lively fire, in a little fat (butter, fat, or oil), while constantly moving the pan, thus making the meat *sauter* to prevent its sticking to the pan.

In this country the expression panfry is sometimes used instead of sauté, but this is misleading. To fry means to use a good portion of fat.

Only tender meat can be sautéed. The meat may be dredged with flour before cooking, but neither liquid nor sauce is added during the cooking period. Meat should always be sautéed in a skillet that has a fairly thick bottom and sides that are not over two inches high. The reason for such a pan is that the meat is cooked over rather high heat—a thin pan might buckle or allow the meat to burn—and high sides on the pan would allow too much moisture to fall back on the meat.

A small amount of fat (usually not over 2 tablespoons in a recipe to serve four) is melted in the skillet. This should get hot but it should not smoke or burn. Only thin slices of tender meat should be used. They should be browned quickly on both sides and if you want the slice to be cooked thoroughly, the heat may be lowered for a few minutes of extra cooking. Do not cover the pan and do not add liquid.

Some meats are sautéed in a slightly different way. For instance, chicken pieces, because of their size, and pork chops, because they should be very thoroughly cooked. Use the same amount of fat as for regular sautéing and brown the meat as stated above. After the meat is browned, the uncovered pan is put in a moderate oven for a period of time to finish the cooking. An alternate method is to cover the skillet and continue the cooking over a moderate heat on the top of the stove. If you use the latter method, the exterior of the meat, of course, will not be crisp. One way to help rectify this is to uncover the pan for the last ten to fifteen minutes of the cooking period.

A sauce is sometimes made, after removing the meat from the pan, by skimming off some of the grease and adding flour and wine or broth (or both), and seasonings.

You will sometimes find recipes with the word sauté in their names which *do* add liquid to the meat after it is browned in fat. This derives from French kitchen language and means that the cooking began with the sautéing process. Such dishes are variations of stews, sometimes quite elaborate.

❀ To Braise

This method of cooking requires liquid, thus providing moist heat. It is used for the less tender cuts of meat. If the meat has little fat of its own, it should be larded. Marinating makes the meat more tender and it improves the flavor. After the meat has been larded and marinated (see Chapter 7), it may or may not be dredged with flour. It is browned in a very little hot fat in a heavy kettle or skillet. If the meat has been marinated, the vegetables of the marinade are added and the marinade, or a portion of it, is poured over the meat and the vegetables. Often the liquid is quickly reduced to a syrupy state by rapid boiling. Baste the meat with the liquid, cover the kettle, reduce the heat to a very slow simmer, and cook on the top of the stove. Or, cook in the oven at a temperature of from 300° to 325°.

If the meat is not first marinated, either a little stock or water is used for liquid, and vegetables and seasonings are often added. The liquid should cover the bottom of the kettle; the meat should not be submerged. If, during the cooking period, it appears to be at all dry, it should be basted with the juices in the bottom of the kettle or, if the amount of liquid does not seem to be sufficient, you may add a little more.

Braising requires a fairly long cooking time, since the heat is kept low (to preserve moisture) and the cuts usually used have considerable connective tissue which must be allowed to break down.

❁ To Stew

This is another method of cooking the less tender cuts. Braising, stewing, and fricasseeing are often confused. They are similar in that they are all moist-heat methods. In stewing, the meat is first cut into uniform pieces, generally two-inch cubes, so that as much surface area as possible is exposed to the liquid. The cubes are usually browned in a little hot fat, although some recipes require that the meat be well heated but not browned. The meat is then covered with liquid (water, stock, or a mixture of stock and wine) and seasonings are added. The liquid is brought to a boil, the pot is covered, and the heat is immediately reduced. Cooking at a simmer may take from one to three hours. Vegetables, if any, are added near the end of the cooking time; the time will vary according to the vegetable. For some stews, at the end of the cooking period, the liquid is thickened.

❁ To Fricassee

To fricassee is to stew—that is, the meat is generally cut into regular pieces, browned or not browned according to the recipe, and simmered in a liquid until tender. The difference between the two is that a fricassee is usually covered with a sauce when it is served. This sauce is usually made from the liquid in which the meat has cooked. The liquid is stirred into flour and butter that have been cooked together for a specified length of time and, possibly, egg yolks and cream are added. Sometimes lemon juice is added. This form of cooking is called *blanquette* in France (see Index for Blanquette of Veal).

❀ To Poach, to Simmer, or to Cook in Water

Usually chicken (a whole mature hen) is poached. The cleaned, dressed fowl is covered with boiling water or stock, the pot is covered, and the chicken is simmered until tender. Vegetables and seasonings are added for flavor.

Cured or corned meats, heart, and tongue, are the meats most often simmered or cooked in water at a low temperature. Cured and corned meats can do without flavoring agents added to the water, although some recipes call for bay leaf and certain spices; fresh cuts are helped by them.

No meat of any kind should ever be *boiled*. Losses of flavor and nutrients are too great and the high heat often breaks apart muscle fibers, completely dissolving connective tissue, thus making the meat stringy and dry. This applies even to soup meat; boiling makes the broth cloudy.

CHAPTER 7

Marinating, Larding, and Cooking with Wine

✿ Marinating

Meat is marinated to improve its flavor and to tenderize it. It is the less tender cuts of meat from the chuck, rump, flank, etc. that marinating helps the most. Meat can be marinated anywhere from a few hours to several days. A cool, airy room is the best place to do this, but you can also marinate meat in your refrigerator. Pork is seldom marinated, though a "dry" marinade, a mixture of herbs and seasonings rubbed into the surface of a roast some time before it is cooked, can be very good (see Index).

BASIC MARINADE

(For a 2- to 4-lb. piece of meat)

1 carrot, sliced
1 large onion, chopped or sliced
1 stalk celery, sliced
1 or 2 cloves of garlic, sliced
2 sprigs parsley

¼ teaspoon dried thyme

½ bay leaf

4 peppercorns, crushed

1 or 2 cloves (optional)

1 cup per 2 lbs. meat of dry white wine (red wine may be used but it tends to change the color of the meat; white wine simply improves the flavor)

¼ cup olive or cooking oil per 2 lbs. of meat

¼ cup lemon juice per 2 lbs. of meat

Season the meat with salt and pepper. If the meat is lean, it may be larded. Use a glass or earthenware bowl just large enough to accommodate the meat and the marinade. Put half of the sliced carrot and onion in the bottom of the bowl. Place the meat on this. Add the remainder of the carrot and onion, all the other flavoring ingredients, then the wine, oil, and lemon juice. Keep the bowl in a cool place or in the refrigerator. Turn the meat often (about every four hours, though you needn't lose any sleep over it!). The top side of the meat should not be allowed to dry out (the oil in the marinade helps to seal the meat from the air). Keep the bowl covered.

When the meat has been marinated the required length of time, remove it from the marinade, and drain it in a large sieve or colander for at least an hour before it is to be cooked. But be sure to check your recipe on this—you may use the marinade in the cooking.

❁ Larding

Although the meat you buy in this country is perhaps the best in the world, there are still certain cuts of meat that are improved by being larded. When marbling is lacking, larding takes its place. Larding is accomplished by drawing through the meat, with a larding needle, tiny strips of pork fat or salt pork. Sometimes the lardoons, as the little strips are called, are rolled in garlic powder and other herbs before they are inserted.

There are actually three methods of larding. One, which consists of drawing long strips of fat through the center of the meat lengthwise (with the grain), is generally too difficult a task to be done at home. Some butchers can and will do this for you. It is rather impressive to see a cut slice of meat on which this type of larding has been done, for the slice will have a pattern of several little squares of fat in it. The other two methods, which I describe below, can be done at home. They do require the use of a manageable needle (the hollow, tubelike kind drawn to a point at one end) or a knife, and only small stitches are made on the surface of the meat.

Meats that have little or no fat covering or internal fat—such as cuts from the round, the rump, sweetbreads, whole beef tenderloins, or meat of U.S. Good grade or below—all have their juiciness and flavor increased if they are larded.

The main problem if you have never larded your meat is one of finding a needle. Unfortunately, larding is becoming a lost art in this country. True, with meat getting better and better there is less and less need for it, but I do think the modern housewife sometimes sacrifices good economy to timesaving. Thus, she may either buy an expensive cut of meat, well-marbled to save herself the time of larding, or she may neglect to lard a very lean, less expensive cut because she thinks it takes too much time. She is mistaken in the latter instance—larding takes about five minutes.

And I have found that needle for you. If the kitchenwares departments of the stores in your town do not have larding needles or cannot get them for you, there is a store in New York City that will sell them by mail order: Bazar Français, 666 Sixth Avenue, New York 10, N. Y. The needles come in various lengths; one measuring either 8⅝ inches or 9½ inches would be best. They are all under a dollar each.

To lard, you first cut the pork fat or salt pork into strips ¾ to 2 inches long and about ⅛ inch thick. Put the strips in the end of the needle, leaving a tiny bit hanging out, and pull the needle through. The strip will stay behind in the meat and a portion of it will probably show above the surface. Repeat this procedure at ½ to 1-inch intervals, depending on the cut of meat and how much fat you want added to it.

A far more time-consuming and less adequate way to lard is to poke a small paring knife into the meat and then to push a piece of pork fat into the cut. It sometimes is difficult to keep the fat in the cut unless the incision is deep. However, if you haven't invested in a larding needle, this method is better than nothing.

In certain instances meat should also be barded, to borrow another word from France. This is the tying of a large sheet of suet or salt pork, or strips of bacon, over or around the meat. When there is no fat covering, barding will take its place. The breasts of poultry to be roasted or the sides of a beef filet often should be barded.

❀ Cooking Meat with Wine

When the reader looks at the recipes in this book—both for meat and the sauces that accompany meat—she (and also he, I hope!) will notice that a good number of them call for wine. If you have never cooked with wine (and I do not consider using "cooking sherry" as cooking with wine), don't just throw up your hands and say such things as "it's too much trouble," "my husband doesn't like fancy food," "I don't drink," or "I can't stand wine." Try it; you will be amazed at how the flavor of meat is enhanced by just a small amount of this wonderful liquid. And, if you have already cooked with wine, you know what I mean.

Most of the recipes in this book that require wine call for either a dry red wine or a dry white wine. You do not by any means have to use imported wine. A modestly priced California wine will do very nicely. Under the heading of dry red wine you will find from California such names on the labels as Burgundy, Pinot Noir, Cabernet, and Mountain Red. Under the heading of dry white wine you will find Pinot Blanc, Dry Semillon, Chablis, Riesling, and Mountain White. Any of these is quite satisfactory and may be better than some of the very inexpensive imported wines. Fine imported wines, of course, are wonderful—and extravagant.

When you have used the amount of wine required for the recipe, what could be better than to serve the remainder of the bottle with the meal? Unless, of course, you are one, as I hinted above, who "doesn't drink" or who "can't stand wine." If this is the case, don't despair—given a few days in a warm kitchen, the wine will turn to vinegar, and vinegar can always be used for cooking or for salad dressing. And remember that the alcohol in wine evaporates completely by the time the dish is cooked.

CHAPTER 8

Sauces for Meat

Brillat-Savarin, who came to this country for several years when, for political reasons, it would have been unhealthy for him to remain in his native France, made the statement that America had one hundred religions and only one sauce. This 150-year-old exaggeration has stuck with us to a certain extent, unfortunately. Just what the sauce was that he was referring to I am not quite sure, but I can retaliate by saying that, when you get right down to it, France has but *two* sauces! These two, the brown sauce and the white sauce, are the bases for the dozens of sauces made today—both in Europe and in the United States.

There are few things better than a tender, juicy porterhouse steak—even without salt and pepper—that comes sizzling from the broiler. Such meat is not really improved by a sauce, although a sauce certainly will do it no harm. But one can't (and, I hope, wouldn't want to) have a steady diet of broiled porterhouse steak. What about the more economical meats—chuck roasts, round steaks, hens? You *do* buy them, I am sure. And how do you cook them? By moist heat. What is in the liquid remaining when these meats have been cooked? All those nitrogenous extractives—literally the flavor of the meat! It is the liquid in the stew, its "sauce," that makes it so good.

A sauce not only enhances so many meats, it also adds variety. How boring to have the same meat day after day unless you can add to and change its flavor with various sauces.

The sauces listed here are made from scratch. When you read the recipes you will find that many can be made with the juices and fat remaining in the pan after the meat has been cooked. Also, if you are an experimental cook, you can try your own hand at variations from the basic brown and white sauces.

The recipes will yield approximately one cup of sauce each. This amount will usually be enough for four to six servings, and may be stretched to eight if not much sauce is desired. A brown sauce should never be so thick as to be pasty; rather it should be on the thin side. A white sauce may be served a little thicker, but it still should never be pasty. However, remember that any pan sauce or gravy thickened with flour or cornstarch must cook lightly for 2 or 3 minutes.

Many of the sauces below, including the Basic Brown Sauce, are household adaptations of classic sauces, the names of which are given in parentheses only to tell you what the original source of the recipe is, should you be curious to know. (The same applies to the white sauces further on.) Out of respect for the august French chefs who created and named these sauces, it is only fair to point out clearly that these recipes *are* adaptations. But the original recipes, as you can well imagine, are usually quite impractical for the everyday American kitchen.

THE BROWN SAUCES

BASIC BROWN SAUCE (SAUCE ESPAGNOLE)

Melt 2 tablespoons of butter in a small saucepan. In it sauté very lightly 1 tablespoon of finely minced onion. Add 2 table-

spoons of flour and mix thoroughly. Cook this mixture very
slowly, stirring constantly, until it is a light brown color. This
should take about 15 minutes. Slowly stir in one 10½-ounce can
of beef broth. Simmer, stirring occasionally, for 25 minutes.
Add 1 heaping tablespoon of tomato paste, and mix until
smooth.

When making any of the variations and elaborations below,
wait until the sauce has been completely made before tasting to
see if salt should be added, since the basic sauce is already
seasoned. If you do not use all of the basic sauce at one time,
the remainder may be stored in a well-sealed glass, plastic, or
earthenware container in the refrigerator for up to two weeks.
And, of course, it is convenient to make a larger amount of this
basic recipe at one time. You can keep it in the refrigerator if
you intend to make a number of sauces in a two-week period.
Or you can freeze it very successfully and have a supply on hand
for up to six months if your freezer maintains a temperature of
0° F. or below.

VARIATIONS AND ELABORATIONS OF THE BROWN SAUCE

Madeira Sauce (*Sauce Madère*): To the Basic Brown Sauce add
2 tablespoons of Madeira at the same time that you add the
tomato paste.

Good with: ham, tongue.

Bordelaise Sauce: Pour 1 cup of dry red or dry white wine into
a saucepan. Add 1 teaspoon of minced green onion, a tiny pinch
a thyme, a sliver of bay leaf, and a pinch of salt. Reduce by
boiling to approximately one half the original volume. Then
add ½ cup of the Basic Brown Sauce and bring just to a boil.
Add 1 tablespoon of butter and strain the sauce through a sieve.

Good with: broiled steaks or hamburger patties, sautéed liver, leftover roast beef or pot roast, broiled or sautéed veal or lamb kidneys, brains.

Mushroom Sauce: Sauté in 2 tablespoons of hot butter ¼ pound of fresh mushrooms, sliced, or 4 ounces of canned mushrooms, drained. Add 1 cup of the Basic Brown Sauce and 1 tablespoon of Madeira.

Good with: chops, steaks, sautéed chicken.

Pork Sauce (*Sauce Charcutière*): Heat 2 tablespoons bacon drippings in a skillet, and in this sauté 2 tablespoons of minced onion. Mix in 1 cup of the Basic Brown Sauce and allow to boil for a few seconds. Add 2 tablespoons of minced dill pickle.

Good with: all cuts of pork.

Hunter's Sauce (*Sauce Chasseur*): Melt 3 tablespoons of butter in a skillet, and in it sauté ½ pound of chopped fresh mushrooms or 8 ounces of canned mushrooms, drained and chopped. Add 1 tablespoon of minced green onion. When the mushrooms and onion are nicely colored, pour over them ½ cup of dry white wine. Boil until volume is reduced by approximately one half. Mix in ½ cup of the Basic Brown Sauce, 1 heaping tablespoon of tomato paste, 1 tablespoon of chopped parsley, a pinch of dried chervil, and a pinch of dried tarragon. Just before serving add 1 tablespoon of butter.

Good with: chops, steaks, hamburger patties, sautéed chicken, sautéed lamb or veal kidneys, leftover roast beef or pot roast.

Tarragon Sauce: Mix together in a saucepan ⅓ cup of dry white wine, 1 tablespoon of minced green onion, and 1 cup of the Basic Brown Sauce. Reduce by boiling to approximately one half the original volume. Remove from the heat and add 4 tablespoons of butter, ¼ teaspoon of dried tarragon (or fresh chopped tarragon to taste), a tiny sprinkle of cayenne, and a squeeze of lemon juice.

Good with: all cuts of beef.

Devil Sauce (*Sauce Diable*): Mix together in a saucepan ½ cup of dry white wine, 1 tablespoon of white-wine vinegar, 1 tablespoon of minced green onion, a tiny pinch of thyme, ¼ bay leaf, and 4 to 6 freshly crushed peppercorns. Reduce by boiling to approximately one half the original volume. Add ⅔ cup of the Basic Brown Sauce, and allow the mixture to boil for a few seconds. Strain the sauce through a sieve, and just before serving stir in 1 teaspoon of chopped parsley and a tiny sprinkle of cayenne.

Good with: broiled chicken, broiled liver, pot roast, sweetbreads, tongue.

Herb Sauce (*Sauce aux Fines Herbes*): Mix together in a sauce pan ⅓ cup of dry white wine, 1 tablespoon of chopped parsley, 1 teaspoon of chopped chives, a pinch of dried chervil, and a pinch of dried tarragon. Boil gently for 2 to 3 minutes. In another saucepan melt 1 tablespoon of butter and in it sauté lightly 1 tablespoon of minced green onion. Add the wine mixture to this, and reduce the entire mixture by boiling to one half its original volume. Add ¾ cup of the Basic Brown Sauce and simmer for about 10 minutes. Just before serving stir in 1 tablespoon of butter and a generous squeeze of lemon juice.

Good with: steaks, chops, sautéed chicken.

Lyonnaise Sauce: Melt 2 tablespoons of butter in a saucepan, and in it sauté until transparent 1 finely chopped onion. Add 2 tablespoons of white-wine vinegar and ¼ cup of dry white wine.

Bring to a slow boil and boil for 5 minutes. Stir in ¾ cup of the Basic Brown Sauce and boil again for 3 to 4 minutes.

Good with: chops, hamburger patties, pork, tongue.

Portuguese Sauce (*Sauce Portugaise*): Heat 1 tablespoon of olive oil in a saucepan, and in it sauté until transparent 1 tablespoon of finely minced onion. Add 3 tomatoes, peeled, seeded, and chopped, and ½ clove of minced garlic. Bring to a boil, cover the pan, reduce the heat, and simmer for 25 minutes, stirring occasionally. Add ½ cup of the Basic Brown Sauce, 1 tablespoon of chopped parsley, and a good pinch of freshly ground black pepper.

Good with: beef, sautéed chicken, braised veal chops, leftover roast beef or pot roast.

Robert Sauce: Melt 1 tablespoon of butter in a saucepan, and in it sauté 2 finely chopped onions until they are transparent. Add ¼ cup of dry white wine and 2 tablespoons of white-wine vinegar. Boil this mixture until it is reduced to approximately one half the original volume. Add 1 cup of the Basic Brown Sauce and 1 tablespoon of tomato paste. Simmer for about 10 minutes. Just before serving stir in 1 tablespoon of prepared mustard.

Good with: beef and pork.

The White Sauces

The basic white sauce, called *sauce béchamel* in France, is not always the basis for all of the white sauces. It would be closer to the truth to say that the basis for the white sauces is "white" stock, either veal or chicken. Veal stock, enriched as it is by gelatin from the veal bones, is the preferred base for sauces for many dishes, even including those for chicken dishes, though this last is a rather special refinement. Since veal stock really is preferable in so many cases, almost all the variations of white sauces below refer either to the Veal Stock recipe or to the Foundation Sauce made with it. Unfortunately, there are no canned veal stocks, or cubes similar to beef bouillon cubes, that I know of. But it is really not difficult to make veal stock, and you will find that the ultimate sauce is better for the little time it takes.

Having said all this in favor of veal stock, however, the fact remains that the substitution of chicken stock as the base for white sauces for meats other than chicken and, of course, for chicken itself, is perfectly acceptable even to some very fussy cooks. In this country one good reason for this is that one can buy very good canned chicken stock, chicken bouillon cubes, or powdered chicken-stock base and spare oneself the making of any stock at all. Therefore, you may read "chicken" for "veal" whenever stock is mentioned in the recipes that will follow.

VEAL STOCK
(Makes about 1 pint)

1 lb. veal shank
3 cups water
1 small carrot
½ onion
½ stalk celery
¼ bay leaf
Small pinch dried thyme
Sprig parsley
Tiny piece clove
½ teaspoon salt

Place the shank in a deep kettle and cover it with the water. Bring to a boil, and after about 5 minutes remove the scum that has risen to the top. Add all the other ingredients and simmer, covered, for 2½ hours. Cool, strain, and pour into a jar for storage. Do not skim off the fat; it will keep out the oxygen and consequently retard souring. (The fat can easily be pulled off in its solid state before the stock is used.) Store, tightly covered, in the refrigerator. The stock will keep about a week; if it is not all used within the week, reheat the remainder to the boiling point, cool, and store again in a covered jar.

FOUNDATION SAUCE

In a saucepan, over low heat, melt 2 tablespoons of butter and stir in 2 tablespoons of flour. Do not allow to brown. Slowly add 1 cup of Veal Stock and cook, stirring constantly, until the sauce coats the spoon.

BÉCHAMEL SAUCE (WHITE SAUCE)

In a saucepan, over low heat, melt 2 tablespoons of butter and stir in 2 tablespoons of flour. Do not allow to brown. Add, slowly, 1¼ cups of scalded milk. Then add ½ teaspoon of minced onion, ¼ teaspoon of salt, a pinch of white pepper, a touch of nutmeg, a tiny pinch of dried thyme, and a sliver of bay leaf. Simmer this mixture for 30 minutes, stirring often. Strain through a sieve.

There are three ways to vary the flavor of your béchamel if the sauce is destined for meat: 1) for veal dishes, save a scrap of the raw veal—enough to make about 2 tablespoonfuls, chopped—and add this along with the onion and seasonings (this is called *béchamel au gras* in classic cuisine and is a handy way to avoid making a veal stock for the white-sauce variations listed below); 2) instead of all milk, use ¼ cup of Veal Stock and 1 cup of scalded milk; 3) for chicken dishes, but for almost any meat dish requiring a white sauce, too, use ¼ cup of chicken stock and 1 cup of scalded milk.

VARIATIONS AND ELABORATIONS OF THE WHITE SAUCE

German Sauce (*Sauce Allemande* or *Sauce Parisienne*): In a heavy saucepan lightly beat 1 egg yolk. Add ⅓ cup of cold Veal Stock. Reduce the liquid from an 8-ounce can of mushrooms to one half its original volume and add 3 tablespoons of this to the egg mixture. In another saucepan melt 1 tablespoon of butter and stir in 1 tablespoon of flour. Slowly add ½ cup of Veal Stock, and when this is thoroughly blended, add it slowly to the egg mixture. Season with a dash of white pepper and nutmeg, and salt if needed. Heat slowly, stirring constantly, until the sauce coats the spoon. Strain through a sieve, and just before serving add 2 tablespoons of butter and a tiny squeeze of lemon juice.

Good with: sweetbreads, poached chicken, brains.

Sunrise Sauce (*Sauce Aurore*): To ⅔ cup of the Foundation Sauce add 2 tablespoons tomato paste. Heat, and at the last minute stir in 2 tablespoons of butter.

Good with: veal chops, sautéed or braised chicken, sweetbreads.

Breton Sauce (*Sauce Bretonne*): Melt 1 tablespoon of butter in a saucepan and in it sauté ½ a finely minced onion and ½ stalk of finely minced celery. Season with a pinch of salt and sugar. When the onion is transparent, add 2 tablespoons minced mushrooms. Sauté for 3 more minutes. Then add ⅓ cup of dry white wine and boil slowly for 5 minutes. Add 1 cup of the Foundation Sauce and boil for a few seconds. At the last minute stir in 2 tablespoons of butter and 1 tablespoon of thick cream.

Good with: veal chops, sautéed or braised chicken, sweetbreads.

Cream Sauce (*Sauce Suprême*): To 1 cup of Béchamel Sauce add ⅓ cup of cream. Reduce the volume by one third by slowly boiling. Just before serving add 2 tablespoons of butter and 3 tablespoons of cream.

Good with: poached chicken, sweetbreads.

Hungarian Sauce (*Sauce Hongroise*): Melt 2 tablespoons of butter in a saucepan and in it lightly sauté 2 tablespoons of minced onion. Stir in 2 tablespoons of flour and ¼ teaspoon Hungarian paprika. Add ½ cup of dry white wine. Season with a dash of salt, a pinch of dried thyme, ¼ bay leaf, and a sprig of parsley. Add 1 cup of Veal Stock and simmer 25 minutes. Strain through a sieve and add 2 tablespoons of butter just before serving.

Good with: veal chops, sautéed, poached, or braised chicken, sweetbreads.

White-Wine Sauce: In a saucepan mix 2 tablespoons of dry white wine, 2 tablespoons of white-wine vinegar, 1 minced green onion (the white part), a tiny pinch of dried thyme, a sliver of bay leaf, a small sprig of parsley, and a pinch each of salt and white pepper. Boil rapidly for 3 minutes and then stir in 1 cup of the Foundation Sauce and ⅓ cup of liquid from canned mushrooms. Boil again and reduce to two thirds the original volume. Strain through a sieve. Just before serving, stir in 4 tablespoons of cream and a sprinkle of cayenne.

Good with: sautéed or braised chicken, sweetbreads.

Curry Sauce (*Sauce à l'Indienne*): Melt 1 tablespoon of butter in a saucepan and in it sauté 1 finely minced onion. Add 1/4 bay leaf, a pinch of dried thyme, and 1 tablespoon of curry powder. Stir in 1/4 cup of chicken stock. Boil for 1 to 2 minutes. Add 1 cup of the Foundation Sauce (made with chicken instead of veal stock) and again boil for 10 minutes. Strain through a sieve and at the last minute stir in 1/3 cup of thick cream.

Good with: sautéed chicken.

Mustard Sauce: To 1 cup of Bechamel Sauce add 2 teaspoons (or more to taste) of dry mustard, 1 teaspoon of prepared mustard, and a sprinkle of Hungarian paprika. Mix well.

Good with: roast pork, braised pork chops.

Horseradish Sauce: To 1 cup of Bechamel Sauce add 1 tablespoon to 1/4 cup (to taste) of prepared horseradish, well drained. Mix well.

Good with: boiled beef or simmered brisket.

CHAPTER 9

The Carving and Serving of Meat

Many things contribute to the success or failure of a dinner party. Success requires congenial guests, an attractively set table, a pleasant pace in the succession of courses, good food—AND neat and relaxed carving of the meat, whether it is done at the table or in the kitchen. To have a husband who is a good meat carver makes a wife proud; and a good job of carving gives a man a satisfying sense of achievement. A messy job, in fact, especially in front of guests, can be positively humiliating.

No one is a born meat carver, nor is the skill magically acquired overnight. Indeed, I have known some excellent surgeons who did not favorably advertise their skills when confronted with a leg of lamb! To carve well takes knowledge of the anatomy of the cut, *sharp* knives (usually the long, rather slim carving knife and the shorter, sturdy boning knife), a steady platter or board, patience, and practice. If one or another of the above is lacking, your chances of arriving at that sense of achievement drop precipitously.

Two sensible trends are in evidence these days—carving the meat in the kitchen and doing it on a large wooden plank especially made for carving. By carving in the kitchen you, of course, deprive the guests of seeing a job well done, if you *can* do it well, but you gain the advantage of being able to forget your dignity and seize a wobbling roast with your hands, if necessary, and to keep everything hot on the stove until you are ready to serve. The best wooden plank is the kind with metal spikes designed to hold the meat firmly in place (which in some planks may be removed when not needed) and a trough to catch the escaping juices. When the carving knife hits the wood there is far less chance of dulling or nicking the blade than when it hits metal, hard china, or pottery.

If the carving is to be done at the table, above all give the carver plenty of room; see that glasses, flatware, and dishes that he will not be using are out of his way. Place the meat platter (or the plank if the dinner is informal), which is *at least* two inches larger all around than the meat served on it, on a non-skid surface directly in front of the carver. Place the serving plate or dinner plates near enough to the platter to avoid having a stream of meat juice land on the table. If garnishes are on the platter with the meat, have them arranged so that last-minute pushing aside is not necessary. A carving knife and fork and a large spoon for the meat juices should all be put on the table near the platter.

Rules for Carving

In the following pages are diagrams of some of the most common meat cuts requiring carving. The dotted lines show how the carving should progress. If problems arise while you are carving, remember these few basic rules:

In large cuts of meat such as roasts, try to cut as much as possible across the grain. (This is often neither necessary nor practical in the carving of very tender steaks.)

When exterior bones are present that can be easily cut out, remove them before cutting the meat. (For preliminary help on location of hidden bones, see the four Bone Charts for beef, veal, lamb, and pork.)

Follow natural divisions of muscles in steaks or pot roasts when these will yield serving portions.

When a roast has been rolled and is held together by string, remove only one or two loops of string at a time; the roast is likely to fall apart if you cut all the string at once.

A sawing motion with the knife yields whole slices, whereas pushing or pulling the knife with no lateral motion tends to yield uneven, crumbly bits.

❀ Standing Rib Roast

When buying this cut, if you have the butcher loosen the backbone from the ribs, the entire backbone may be removed as "step one" in carving. Next you have the choice of two methods to carve individual slices. The method pictured here is best for small roasts and may also be used on one of any size:

Step 2

Step 2: Start at the outer edge of the fat and cut in to the rib, as the dotted line shows, making an even slice about three eighths of an inch thick. (This thickness is what I prefer; you can "stretch" a roast by slicing thinner if you wish. Whatever thickness you prefer, the important thing is the evenness of the slice.) Hold the roast steady by inserting the fork in the side,

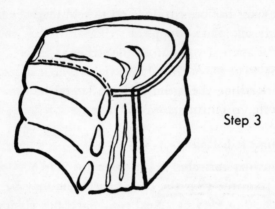

Step 3

between the top two ribs. **Step 3:** Free the slice by cutting down right next to the rib and remove the slice to a plate. **Step 4:** Remove the rib when you begin cutting slices below it.

The other method is best for large roasts only:

Step 2: Remove all the ribs at once (the backbone is already removed, as above), thus yielding a completely boneless cut. **Step 3:** Turn the roast so that the part from which the ribs have just been removed rests on the platter. **Step 4:** Quickly, with short sawing strokes, cut the slices off downward, holding the roast steady with the fork.

❀ Rolled Rib Roast

Place the roast on the platter or board with the smaller cut end facing up. Hold the roast steady with the fork, inserting the tines in the *side,* about an inch below the intended size of the slice. **Step 1:** Remove one loop of string. If the roast has been rolled properly, the string will be continuous throughout most of the cut and it will pierce the fat in a line down one side. You will have to cut the string here and carefully remove any little pieces of it remaining after you have cut the slice. **Step 2:** With a steady sawing motion, cut slices about three eighths of an inch thick and remove them to a plate.

✿ Porterhouse or T-bone Steak

Step 1: Remove the bone, preferably with a small knife or boning knife, by cutting along the lean right next to it. **Step 2:** Make individual serving portions by cutting with a sawing motion clear across the steak. When you reach the "tail," make fanning slices as indicated in the diagram.

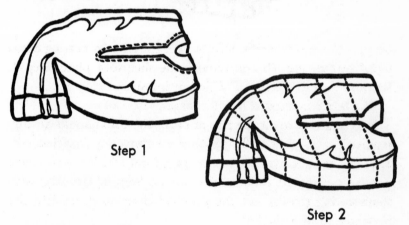

Step 1

Step 2

✿ Sirloin Steak

The carving of this steak is much the same as that of the porterhouse. Remove the bones first. Since there are several different muscles in the sirloin section, change the direction of the knife so that the meat fibers are cut as short as possible; that is, try to cut across the grain in the larger muscles. A pin-bone sirloin steak poses some problem because the pelvic bone is surrounded by meat; it is often easier to leave this bone in the steak until you make cuts up to it.

❀ Bladebone Pot Roast

The main goal in carving this cut is to make slices across the grain. Since the cut is always braised, the individual muscles are readily separated. **Step 1:** With a boning knife cut one corner off

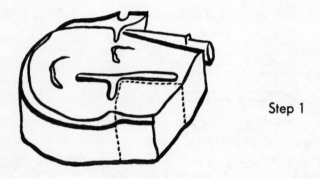

Step 1

close to the bone as pictured, and remove this muscle. **Step 2:** Turn the separated muscle on its side, hold it firmly with a fork, and slice down across the grain. **Step 3:** Proceed as above with the other muscles.

❀ Pork Loin Roast

When buying this cut, if you have the meat cutter loosen the backbone from the ribs, the entire backbone may be removed as the first step in carving. **Step 2:** Place the roast with the rib ends up as pictured and slice downward to make chop-sized

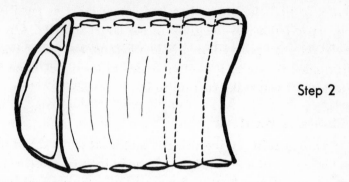

Step 2

servings. If you want, you may cut some slices thin, and without a bone, between the bones.

Whole Ham

The diagrams here show an X-ray view of the ham. By checking the Pork Bone Chart (Chapter 13), you can see that the bones in the ham are part of the hipbone, the leg bone, and part of the shank bone. The leg bone divides the ham lengthwise into two unequal portions, as you can see in the diagram or in the photograph on p. 256.* **Step 1:** Turn the ham on its side

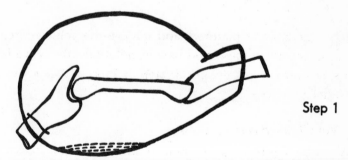

Step 1

* With the shank bone on your right, the thicker side of the ham will be facing you if you have bought a right leg, the thinner side will be facing you if you have bought a left leg.

and cut several lengthwise slices to form a base on which to rest the ham during the remainder of the carving. **Step 2:** Stand the ham on this base, and cut out a wedge-shaped piece from the shank end just inside the knuckle. **Step 3:** Cut several slices down to the bone, starting from where the wedge has been removed. **Step 4:** Insert the knife in the meat at the wedge space and saw along the leg bone, freeing the several slices all at once.

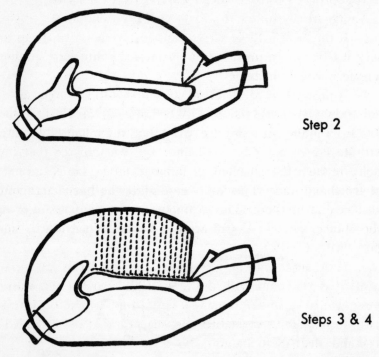

Step 2

Steps 3 & 4

❁ Leg of Lamb

This cut may be carved as the ham is carved since it contains the same bones and has the same structure. The cut is, however, slightly more difficult to carve because of its smaller size and the softer consistency of the meat.

THE SERVING OF MEAT

The most luscious cut of prime beef will be unappetizing and maybe even unsavory if it is served, for instance, lukewarm and half submerged in potatoes and assorted vegetable juices. And, on the other hand, a cut of meat you think might not be too enticing to your family can, surprisingly, really appeal if you serve it properly cooked, hot, and attractively garnished.

Always, always follow these rules when serving meat:

1. If the meat is to be served hot, be sure it *is* hot. Help to keep it that way by putting it on a warmed platter and serving it onto warmed plates.

2. If the meat is to be served cold, it should be refrigerated but not served so cold that it is robbed of its flavor. Never allow it to swim in the sauce or juice of hot food you might be serving with it.

3. Be sure that broiled or roasted meats are as evenly browned and uniform in color as possible—no burns here and uncooked spots there. This is important for flavor as well as appearance, whether the meat is to be served garnished, ungarnished, or with a sauce.

4. If the meat is to be served garnished—and you can be as creative as you want with the ever-faithful parsley and water cress, broiled or stuffed tomatoes, sautéed mushroom caps, tiny balls of potatoes or vegetables, etc.—be sure that the garnish is neat and adequate in amount.

5. If the meat is to be served with a sauce poured over it, be sure that the serving dish is large enough and that the sauce is neat. The sauce should not look like a small ocean making breakers over the edge of the platter.

6. If the meat is to be served with a sauce apart, in a gravy

boat, be sure the sauce is *hot* or *cold,* as the recipe requires. Use dinner plates large enough to allow room for the sauce to be poured over the meat and not over the entire contents of the plate as well.

7. If the meat is to be served sliced, be sure the slices are of uniform thickness, be they thick or thin, and that one slice is not almost all fat and next almost all lean.

PART II

*How Meat Is Cut
and
How to Cook It*

CHAPTER 10

BEEF

The beef you eat comes from cattle especially raised for marketing as meat. It is the weight and shape of these animals, and their ability to mature at an early age, that make them suitable for prospective beef. Herefords, the red-brown cattle with white faces and white undersides; Aberdeen Angus, the sleek black cattle; and Shorthorns, the roans and reds with irregular white markings, are three of the more familiar breeds that end up on your dinner table.

Beef comes from five classes: steers—males castrated when very young; heifers—females that have never borne a calf; cows—mature females that have borne at least one calf; bulls—males that have reached full maturity; and stags—males castrated after maturity. The meat from steers, heifers, and cows is generally, if not always, the meat you eat. High-grade beef usually comes from cattle weighing anywhere from 900 to 1300 pounds each, and the animals usually range in age from one to three years. Regional preferences generally dictate what size carcass is shipped where.

BEEF BONE CHART

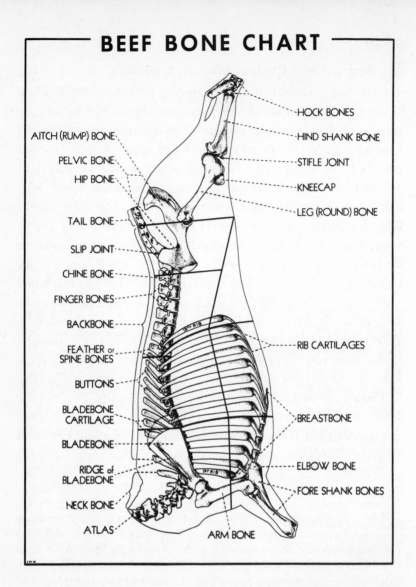

HOCK BONES

HIND SHANK BONE

STIFLE JOINT

KNEECAP

LEG (ROUND) BONE

AITCH (RUMP) BONE

PELVIC BONE

HIP BONE

TAIL BONE

SLIP JOINT

CHINE BONE

FINGER BONES

BACKBONE

FEATHER or SPINE BONES

BUTTONS

BLADEBONE CARTILAGE

BLADEBONE

RIDGE of BLADEBONE

NECK BONE

ATLAS

ARM BONE

RIB CARTILAGES

BREASTBONE

ELBOW BONE

FORE SHANK BONES

❁ Beef of Good Quality: What to Look for

First, check to see if there is a covering of fat over the exterior of the cut. This fat should be firm—you should not be able to press your finger almost through it to the lean—and it should have a somewhat brittle consistency. The color of the fat should usually be a creamy white, although some fat may have a slight yellow tinge. If the fat is a little yellow, be sure that good characteristics of the lean and bone are present. The lean should have a velvety texture, it should be firm to the touch, and it should have a fine grain. Its color can range from pale red to deep red (this variation is due in part to the age of the animal), but it should be bright and uniform. Meat that has remained on display too long will look dry and its color will be an almost brownish red. (If you ask your meat cutter to cut a steak or a roast especially for you, don't be alarmed by the color when he shows it to you. Beef is always dark and almost purple when first cut. After brief exposure to the air it will turn red.)

The extent of marbling—that is, the little "veins" of fat in the lean itself—of course will vary with the cut as well as with the grade: Cuts from the loin, rib, and chuck should be well marbled; cuts from the rump and round should have a fair degree of marbling, though the texture of the meat is more important here.*

* In the future it may become necessary for you to be aware of an artificial method of marbleizing meat. The chief purpose of this is to economize on the large amount of feed and long period of time necessary to fatten cattle to the point where it will produce well-marbleized meat. Fat is injected into the meat after butchering, and a possible advantage will be that vegetable fats as well as animal fats can be used, thus lowering the content of animal fat in meat as some dietary research indicates might be wise. In appearance artificial marbleizing is very convincing and meat treated in this fashion has been sold commercially in a few test areas.

Cuts from the chuck should not have a large amount of intermuscular fat. You would pay for it, but chances are you would not eat it. If you buy a blade cut, p. 123, the scapula (bladebone) should be white and the outer covering should be slightly cartilaginous (smooth and glossy). An arm roast, p. 126, should have a bone that is still somewhat red and porous.

The outside of the rib section should have a gradually sloping contour; it should not make a roller-coaster dip in the area over the rib "eye" muscle. This is the largest muscle of the rib section and comprises most of the lean meat; it should be ample in size and oval in shape and it should not have a squashed appearance (see standing rib, p. 117).

When you are buying a steak from the loin section, check the somewhat large deposit of fat between the main lean muscle and the "tail" (see porterhouse steak, p. 109). The fat should be white, hard, and brittle (it is called the channel fat). The bones in the steak should not be too flinty but rather porous and red.

❀ How Beef Is Cut

At the packing house the beef carcass is divided lengthwise. Each half is called a side. There is often further division into forequarters and hindquarters for convenience in transportation. Forequarters and hindquarters vary a little in different parts of the country. In Philadelphia, for instance, the hindquarter has no ribs; in Chicago one rib is left on the hindquarter, while in Boston the hindquarter will have three ribs. The charts in this book show the Chicago style of cutting.

Unfortunately, the Beef Bone Chart on p. 92 is not three-dimensional, but you can see where the wholesale cuts are made, along the heavy black lines, and where the bones are located in these cuts. If you study this chart and the Beef Cut

BEEF CUT CHART

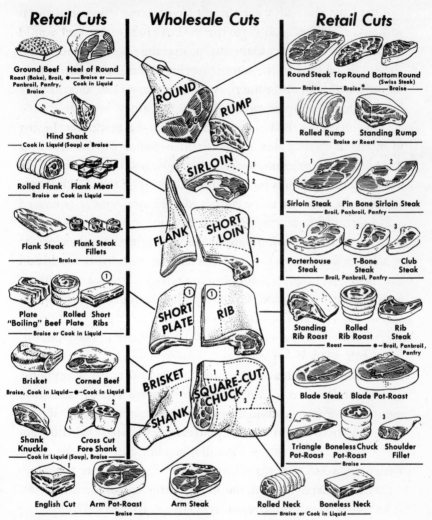

Retail Cuts

Ground Beef
Roast (Bake), Broil, ●—
Panbroil, Panfry,
Braise

Heel of Round
—Braise or
Cook in Liquid

Hind Shank
—Cook in Liquid (Soup) or Braise —

Rolled Flank   Flank Meat
— Braise or Cook in Liquid —

Flank Steak   Flank Steak Fillets
— Braise —

Plate   Rolled   Short
"Boiling" Beef   Plate   Ribs
— Braise or Cook in Liquid —

Brisket   Corned Beef
Braise, Cook in Liquid—●—Cook in Liquid

Shank Knuckle   **Cross Cut Fore Shank**
— Cook in Liquid (Soup), Braise —

English Cut   Arm Pot-Roast   Arm Steak
— Braise —

Wholesale Cuts

ROUND
RUMP
SIRLOIN
FLANK
SHORT LOIN
SHORT PLATE
RIB
BRISKET
SQUARE-CUT CHUCK
SHANK

Retail Cuts

Round Steak Top Round Bottom Round
(Swiss Steak)
— Braise — Braise * — Braise —

Rolled Rump   Standing Rump
— Braise or Roast —

Sirloin Steak   Pin Bone Sirloin Steak
— Broil, Panbroil, Panfry —

Porterhouse Steak   T-Bone Steak   Club Steak
— Broil, Panbroil, Panfry —

Standing Rib Roast   Rolled Rib Roast   Rib Steak
— Roast —   ●—Broil, Panbroil, Panfry

Blade Steak   Blade Pot-Roast

Triangle Pot-Roast   Boneless Chuck Pot-Roast   Shoulder Fillet
— Braise —

Rolled Neck   Boneless Neck
— Braise or Cook in Liquid —

*Prime and choice grades may be broiled, panbroiled or panfried

NATIONAL LIVE STOCK AND MEAT BOARD

Chart showing how the retail beef cuts are made from the wholesale cut, it will help you to understand the descriptions of the retail cuts that follow.

There is some variation in retail cuts across the country. In and around New York City, for example, the sirloin section is divided into two pieces; the end nearest the flank is called the sirloin tip. Because the meat is cut in this fashion, the sirloin steaks are smaller. In some parts of the country the meat cutters remove more bone from the cuts before they are put in the counter. Even in certain sections of a city the meat may be cut in different ways; the markets generally buy and cut their meat according to the demands of the neighborhood or the shopping population. Certain foreign customs, local tradition, or the average size of families are determining factors.

If you move to a new section of the country, or even to a new neighborhood in your city, a careful look at the display counter of a large meat market should tell you what you will be able to buy already cut that is familiar to you. An unfamiliar cut is easily enough identified if you ask the meat cutter what *wholesale* cut it comes from and, if you want to be particularly careful, what *part* of the wholesale cut. By referring to the charts in this book you will be able to tell accurately enough what you are getting and what to do with it. There are also many local variations across the country in the *names* of retail cuts—too many, in fact, to survey usefully in this book. Again, if you establish their origin in the wholesale cut, you can translate accurately enough, and the retail cut will often turn out to be something you are perfectly familiar with by another name.

If the market does not have the cut you want, and if you know your meat, the meat cutter will usually be willing to cut something especially to your order. Be prepared, though, to know more than just the given name of the cut; you must know where it comes from and how it is cut. If you become a real expert, you could go so far as to have a whole side of beef cut to your specifications, regardless of whether the meat cutter is accustomed to doing things your way or not. This is quite an undertaking; you would probably do it only if you were planning to freeze a large quantity of meat, and it could require a forceful personality to achieve the desired results. But you would get what you wanted!

In the descriptions of cuts throughout this book I shall describe mainly the Chicago style of cutting. Use the charts as your point of departure to establish the differences, if there are any, that exist in your locality. The Beef Bone Chart will also identify for you the bones mentioned in the text that follows.

HINDQUARTER

ROUND—Wholesale Cut

This is one of the less tender cuts of the carcass. Much of the lean is not too tender, but there is a good amount of it in proportion to the amount of fat and bone. The retail cuts in the round are:

Round Steak (full cut). Oval in shape (see next page), this cut contains a small round bone, the cross section of the femur, or leg bone. (a) One large muscle. It is the muscle on the inside of the leg and is the most tender of the round-steak muscles. (b) The "eye" muscle of the round. When a round steak is cut into "top" and "bottom" (see below), this muscle is sometimes removed. Do not confuse it with the tenderloin; the grain of this round muscle is much coarser and it is the least tender one in the round. (c) A not too tender muscle; you can notice the difference when you cook the steak, since it will take a longer time to become tender than muscles (a) and (d).

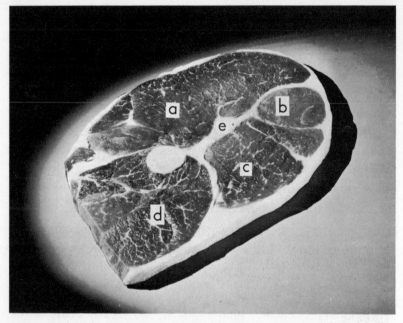

ROUND STEAK (full cut)

(d) This is the muscle that goes over the knee. A portion of it is included in the roast called sirloin tip. (e) As the cuts descend the leg, this fat increases in size. Many markets will remove it entirely when it becomes large, hence the hole you sometimes see in the middle of a round steak. There are about fourteen round steaks per leg, the number depending on how thick they are cut.

To cook: Round steak should be braised. Have your meat cutter pound the steak for you; or pound it yourself with the edge of a plate, the blunt edge of a knife, or a heavy biscuit cutter; or, if it is of especially high quality, cook it unpounded. If you pound the steak yourself, sprinkle the sides first with flour, salt, and pepper so that these will be pushed into the meat.

Simply season and dredge with flour if the steak is not pounded. Heat a little fat in a heavy skillet, brown the steak in it on both sides over medium-high heat, add a little liquid (not enough to submerge the steak), cover, and simmer until the steak is tender. The cooking time will be 1½ to 2½ hours, depending on the size and thickness of the meat.

Onion slices may be browned with the steak. Rounds of carrot and slices of celery may be added to the liquid, which need not be water—try bouillon, dry red or white wine, or a mixture of either of these with water. This general method of braising can be used for all cuts of beef for braising, or see also p. 134.

TOP ROUND STEAK

(a) This is the same muscle as (a) in the whole round steak, the inside leg muscle. If the cut is especially fine looking, with a good amount of marbling and a fine grain, it can be broiled, sautéed, or panfried. However, this cut is usually braised in the same way as a full-cut round steak.

BOTTOM ROUND STEAK

(b) This is the same muscle as (b) in the whole round steak, the round "eye" muscle. (c) The same as (c) in the whole round steak. The bottom round should always be braised. If the cut is thick enough, it becomes a "roast" and will make a good pot roast (see Index for Marinated Pot Roast).

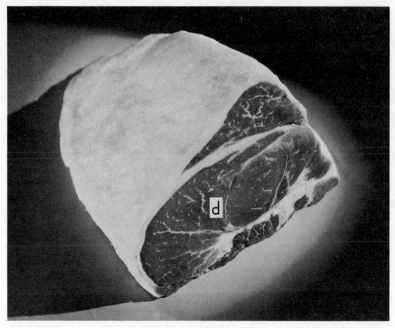

SIRLOIN TIP

If this triangular cut is from a high grade of beef, it can be roasted (see standing rib, p. 118), but it is a good cut to braise; the juices will make a fine base for a sauce. (d) This is the muscle that originates in the round, passing over the knee and on into the lower sirloin section. The cut is sometimes called a knuckle roast.

Heel of the Round. (See photograph on next page.) This is the least tender cut from the round. It is a boneless cut that comes from the back of the leg behind the tibia, or hind shank bone. The muscles are much used by cattle (naturally) and they are separated by thick connective tissue. When some of the

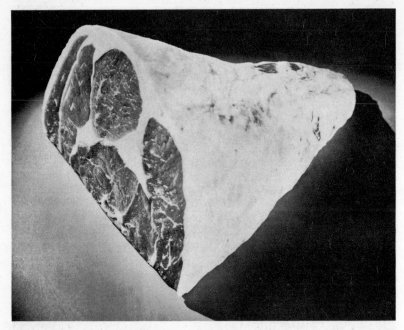

HEEL OF THE ROUND

connective tissue is cut away, the lean makes very good stew meat, rich in extractives. Often a meat cutter will completely cut up the heel of the round before putting it in his counter; some of it will appear as stew meat and the rest as ground beef.

Hind Shank. The tibia (which makes up over 50 per cent of the cut), surrounded by lean and connective tissue. This cut is rich in extractives and is a natural soupbone. It will contain the stifle joint.

RUMP—Wholesale Cut

This is a triangular cut which contains the knucklebone at the end of the femur, the aitch, or rump, bone (one end of the pelvic bone), and the tail bone. You can buy the retail cut in two ways:

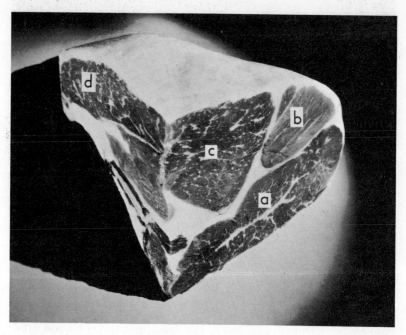

STANDING RUMP

This cut can be quite heavy, not only because of its size, but because of the amount of bone it contains. Even though the knucklebone is usually removed, the rump bone and tail bone remain. These make the cut somewhat difficult to carve. (a), (b), and (c) can be recognized as the same (a), (b), and (c) in the full-cut round steak. (d) This side of the muscle is beginning to resemble the sirloin steak, which is the next cut. Again, if this cut is from high-quality beef, it may be roasted in the same manner as a standing rib; otherwise it should be braised. Braising time will be 3 to 4 hours.

ROLLED RUMP

This is the better way to buy a rump roast. A good meat cutter
will remove all the bones, the undesirable connective tissue,
and the tendons. He will then flatten the fat so it will be of
even thickness to cover two thirds of the cut. And he will sew
the cut with string, piercing the fat and lean so that the cut will
be compact during cooking. You need not buy an entire rolled
rump roast. Once it is sewed, it can be divided into smaller
roasts; and if it is rolled correctly, the grain in each smaller cut
will go all in the same direction, which facilitates carving. A
rolled rump may be cooked in the same way as a standing rump.

SIRLOIN or LOIN END—Wholesale Cut

This cut lies between the round and rump and the short loin. It is the cut which produces all the sirloin steaks. These steaks differ in appearance according to where they are cut. As you can see on the Beef Bone Chart, the pelvic bone and the backbone are contained in sirloin steaks. If the sirloin tip has been removed, only the upper two thirds, approximately, of the wholesale cut will be present, giving you the more tender portion. The sirloin cut terminates at what is called the pinbone, that is, the foremost edge of the pelvic bone. Each steak is named for the shape of the bone it contains, and there can be ten or more steaks per wholesale cut, depending on the size of the carcass and the thickness of the steaks.

Wedge-Bone Sirloin. The largest of the sirloin steaks and the first cut (starting from the rear of the animal). Some of the muscles are cut with the grain, a somewhat undesirable feature. If you will look at the Beef Bone Chart you will see that the wedge bone is the thick, strong part of the pelvic bone just forward of the point where the leg bone is attached.

Round-Bone Sirloin. (See photograph on next page.) Again look at the Beef Bone Chart, and you will see that the pelvic bone becomes smaller and round before it flares out to the slip joint. (a) The round bone.

Double-Bone Sirloin. This steak contains a slice of the pelvis and a portion of the backbone, hence the name. The proportion of bone to lean in this cut is considerably higher than in the wedge- and round-bone sirloin steaks.

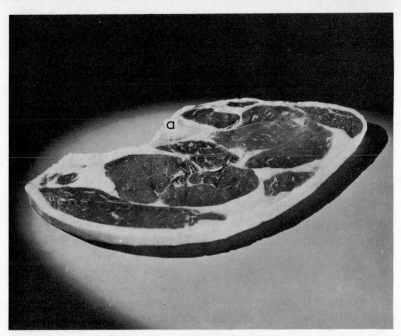

ROUND-BONE SIRLOIN

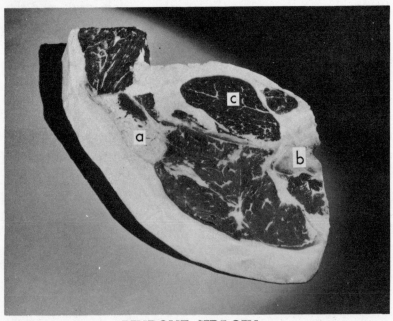

PINBONE SIRLOIN

Pinbone Sirloin. This steak somewhat resembles a porterhouse steak. It lies right next to the porterhouse but contains almost double the amount of bone. (a) The pinbone (hipbone), or the foremost end of the pelvis. (b) Part of the backbone. (c) The tenderloin muscle makes its appearance.

Since the cutting of sirloin steaks varies somewhat in different sections of the country, it is almost impossible to say which cut of steak from the sirloin is the most economical or the best to buy. The safest criterion to follow in buying a sirloin steak is to check the amount of bone (steaks cut at too great a slant will have more bone because of the shape of the pelvis), and check the amount of fat, the amount of marbling, and the direction of the grain (for easier carving, the more the muscles are cut against the grain, the better).

Sirloin steaks may be broiled or panbroiled, but if you intend to broil your steak, it should be at least an inch thick.

Broiling: As I stated earlier in Chapter 6, broiling times are only approximate. Thickness, the amount of bone and fat, the amount of surface area (a larger steak requires a little more time), broiling temperature, and the degree of doneness desired —all these are involved in determining the length of cooking time. You may have noticed variation in cooking times if you own more than one cookbook! Below I offer the timing I have arrived at from my own experience for broiling a sirloin steak; see p. 47 for guidance on broiling frozen steaks.

Broiling times for sirloin steaks:

	Rare		Medium	
		Minutes per Side		
Thickness	*At 350°*	*At high heat*	*At 350°*	*At high heat*
1 inch	10	5-6	12	6-7
1½ inches	15	9-10	17	10-12
2 inches	20	17	22	18-20

Over 2 inches: Sear each side and then cook at 350° for 20 minutes per side; test,* and cook longer if necessary.

Panbroiling: It would be rather ridiculous to suggest panbroiling a huge sirloin steak, but if you have a steak under an inch thick or only a part of a steak, panbroiling is your method. Because the cut will be smaller and thinner, cut the broiling times in the chart above in half for an estimate of the length of panbroiling time.

SHORT LOIN—Wholesale Cut

The short loin is the section between the sirloin and the ribs. Sometimes this section will include the last, or thirteenth, rib, and sometimes it won't—according to where you live. This is the "classy" cut of the carcass, for it contains the porterhouse, the T-bone, and the club steaks.

* See the section on broiling in Chapter 6.

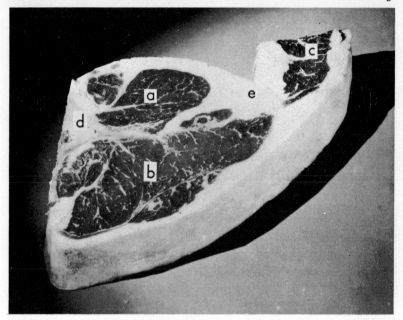

PORTERHOUSE STEAK

The steak of steaks! Named thus because the manner of cutting it originated in a porter (a type of ale) house in England. Be sure never to confuse a pinbone sirloin with a porterhouse; you'll end up with a lot more bone and less tenderloin muscle. Check by looking at both sides of the steak before you buy it. (a) The tenderloin muscle. (b) The loin "eye" muscle. (c) The tail of the steak; less tender than the other two muscles. (d) The bone—the large part is called a chine bone (the body of the vertebra), and the part extending into the steak is called the finger bone (farther up the animal the finger bone turns into a rib). (e) This large amount of fat found in the pinbone sirloin and the porterhouse is called channel fat; it is excellent fat and adds a nice flavor to the meat. A short loin yields about two to three true porterhouse steaks each cut one inch thick, so you can see one big reason why these steaks are usually very expensive. Broiling times:

| | Minutes per Side | | | |
| | Rare | | Medium | |
Thickness	At 350°	At high heat	At 350°	At high heat
1 inch	10	4-5	12	6-7
1½ inches	15	8-9	17	10-11
2 inches	20	13-14	22	17-18

Over 2 inches: Sear each side and then cook at 350° for 20 minutes per side; test,* and cook longer if necessary.

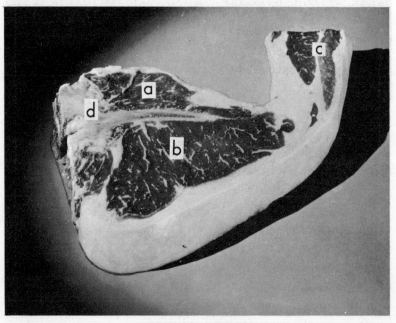

T-BONE STEAK

These steaks follow the porterhouse. (a) The tenderloin is getting smaller. (b) The loin "eye" muscle. (c) The tail is still

* See the section on broiling in Chapter 6.

there, but it too becomes smaller. (d) The reason for the name—
the finger bone is long and the big chine bone forms the cross
of the T. T-bone steaks are smaller in size than the porterhouse
steak, which often makes them a smarter buy if you plan to
have one steak per serving. They are often less expensive than
the porterhouse also. Per short loin, there are usually six or
seven T-bone steaks cut one inch thick.

Broiling times should be the same as for porterhouse steaks.

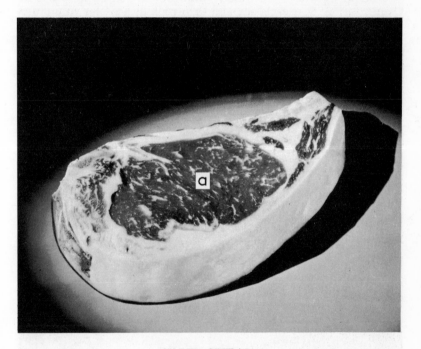

CLUB STEAK

The last cuts in the short loin. (a) The loin "eye" muscle. The
tenderloin has disappeared. The club steak is small—again a
good steak to buy if you plan one steak per serving. There are

about two one-inch-thick club steaks per short loin. Broiling times:

	Minutes per Side			
	Rare		Medium	
Thickness	At 350°	At high heat	At 350°	At high heat
1 inch	7	4-5	10	6-7
1½ inches	12	8-9	15	10-11
2 inches	17	13-14	22	17-18

The porterhouse, the T-bone, and the club steaks may also be panbroiled, especially if they are small or thin. Follow the directions for panbroiling sirloin steaks.

TENDERLOIN

The 3- to 6-pound muscle begins in the sirloin and it ends at the rib end of the short loin. It is the least used muscle in the animal and hence, the most tender. Some say it does not have much flavor (because it is little used, it does not acquire the nitrogenous extractives), but its lack of fat and bone plus the tenderness make it a nice piece of meat. In many European countries the tenderloin is always removed in one piece from the carcass (it is called the *filet*), and the loin "eye" muscle is also removed in one piece (it is called the *faux filet,* or false filet). In this country it is usual *not* to remove either the tenderloin or loin "eye" from wholesale cuts of high-grade beef. It is, instead, from the lower grades of beef that these filets are sometimes removed to be sold as retail cuts. This lower grade makes no difference, however, as the tenderloin, particularly, is tender no matter what grade of beef it is taken from.

To cook: Prepare a tenderloin for cooking by removing any excess fat, sinews, or connective tissue appearing on the surface. A whole tenderloin should be roasted or braised. Because of the lack of fat, it should be larded with salt pork, or barded with fat or bacon strips (see Chapter 7), or the meat should be basted with butter throughout the cooking. For both roasting and braising the temperature of the oven should be 325°. No matter what the weight of the tenderloin, the cooking time should be no longer than 40 minutes. A tenderloin should not be cooked to the well-done stage. For best results when roasting, preheat the oven and use a meat thermometer: It will register 140° when the meat is rare, and 160° when it is medium rare. Mushrooms sautéed in butter are an excellent accompaniment to this cut. (For Braised Beef Filet see Index.)

Filet Mignon or Sliced Tenderloin. The tenderloin is often sliced into various thicknesses, as can be seen in the photograph of the tenderloin. A filet mignon may vary in weight from 4 to

10 ounces. These slices are usually flattened a little at the meat market, but you can ask your meat cutter not to do this. Many European meat recipes call for slices taken from particular sections of the tenderloin, such as filets mignons (small) or tournedos (larger).* These slices make nice individual servings.

* To compare the way meat is cut in America with the way it is cut in Europe is far from easy. For instance, even the filet mignon, which is cut here presumably as it is in France, is not necessarily quite the same, slice for slice. The French actually have five names for different sections of the tenderloin, including the one called tournedos, and only the slices from one of these sections are authentic filets mignons. This is but a minor variation compared to the essential difference, which is that French and other Continental butchers cut a side of beef (and the other meats, also) generally in the direction in which the muscles run. But, as you can see on the Beef Cut Chart, the American method divides the side mostly *across* the muscles. The two systems yield cuts that can be only more or less comparable, never really equivalent. In England, the side is cut generally as it is here, but the terminology is nevertheless very different.

If you happen to want to use cookbooks that were written abroad, the specifications for the cut of meat in a recipe are quite likely to be incomprehensible, even if the book is in English! I know of only three sources that discuss comparable cuts for the United States and Europe effectively: *French Provincial Cooking* by the English author, Elizabeth David, with an introduction and notes to the American edition (Harper & Row) by Narcissa G. Chamberlain; here you will find a succinct chart naming equivalent or comparable cuts for England, France, and the United States. The English-language edition of the famous *Larousse Gastronomique* (Crown) does essentially the same thing in the form of pictorial charts in addition to its discussion of specific cuts in the text. *Mastering the Art of French Cooking* by Beck, Bertholle, and Child (Knopf) discusses French cuts recipe by recipe and gives clear instructions for substituting American cuts.

They may be broiled or sautéed, but care must be taken not to let them dry out; use plenty of butter. Broil under a high heat:

Thickness	*Minutes per Side*	
	Rare	*Medium*
1 inch	2-3	3-4
1½ inches	4-5	5-6
2 inches	5-6	7-8

Or sauté quickly over a high heat, being careful to keep the center rare.

FLANK—Wholesale Cut

As you can see on the Beef Bone Chart, the flank contains as its only bone a portion of the thirteenth rib. Only about 35 per cent of the wholesale cut is lean meat and almost 65 per cent is fat.

Flank Steak. (See photograph on next page.) This is the main edible portion of the flank (enclosed by dotted lines on the Beef Cut Chart). It is a thin, flat, extremely lean and tough cut of meat; do not let the name "steak" deceive you. You will see it in the meat market most often scored as it is in the photograph. This scoring cuts through some of the muscle fibers to help tenderize the steak. This process is necessary because the grain runs lengthwise in the steak.

A flank steak is often stuffed, rolled, and braised (see Index for Stuffed Flank Steak). The stuffing adds flavor and, when rolled, the steak can be cut in slices against the grain. Cooking time should be from 1½ to 2 hours.

Flank steak filets—small slices rolled and held with wooden skewers—should also be braised.

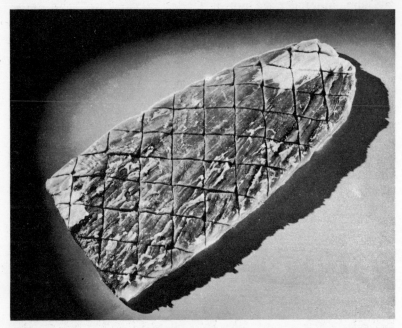

FLANK STEAK

FOREQUARTER

RIB—Wholesale Cut

This cut usually contains seven ribs—from the twelfth down through the sixth—although in some sections of the country it will also contain the thirteenth rib and, also, some meat markets will leave the sixth rib on the chuck. The rib "eye" muscle is the large muscle in this cut (it is the same muscle as the loin "eye"). It is largest at the thirteenth or twelfth rib and slowly decreases in size to the scapula, or bladebone. Contrariwise, the face of the cut increases in size as it approaches the scapula. Small outer muscles contribute to this increase in size. These

muscles, however, are not as tender as the "eye" and consequently do not survive the roasting process as nicely as the
"eye." At the lower, thin section of the rib a cut is made to
produce the short ribs.

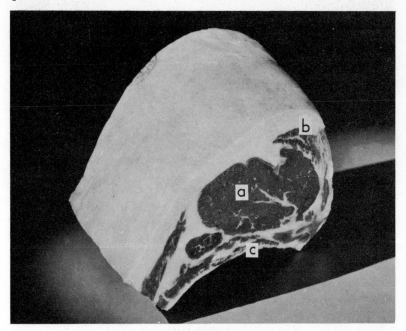

STANDING RIB

This cut, or a portion of it, is often misnamed "Prime rib." A
rib is only Prime if it comes from the Prime grade of beef.
Some persons may think of prime rib as signifying the first ribs
of the section. This also is incorrect, since the ribs are numbered
the other way around, rib number one being up near the arm
bone. (a) The rib "eye" muscle. (b) A small outer muscle (there
are more farther up the cut). (c) The rib. A standing rib roast
usually contains at least two ribs and weighs at least 4 pounds.

The beauty of a rib roast is its ability to stand on its ribs, thus providing its own rack and allowing the exterior fat to baste it while cooking. A roast must have at least two or three ribs to stand by itself. For easier carving, ask your meat cutter to separate the backbone from the ribs, so that the backbone may be easily removed in the kitchen after roasting. It is unwise to buy this cut for a family of two unless you are dying for a good supply of cold roast beef. On the other hand, it is a good cut to buy, especially for quality's sake, if you are planning to serve a fairly large group.

To roast: Prepare a standing rib for roasting by seasoning it if you wish and place it in a roasting pan. For a somewhat shortened cooking time, let the meat stand at room temperature at least an hour before putting it in the oven. Insert a meat thermometer so it goes half way through the "eye" muscle. The thermometer must never rest in fat or on bone. Bone is too good a conductor of heat and fat is a poor conductor. It is the temperature of the lean that you want to gauge. Preheat the oven at 325°. The roast will be rare when the thermometer registers 140°, medium at 160°, and well done at 170°. The cooking time will vary according to the size of the cut, a larger roast requiring less time. Count on approximately 18-20 minutes per pound for a rare roast, 22-25 minutes per pound for a medium roast, and 27-30 minutes per pound for a well-done roast (what a pity!). Use the searing or all-day method if you like (see p. 55).

You may use the fat and drippings as the base for a flour-thickened gravy, but in my opinion it is much better to remove most of the fat from the pan juices and pour these over the meat or into a gravy boat.

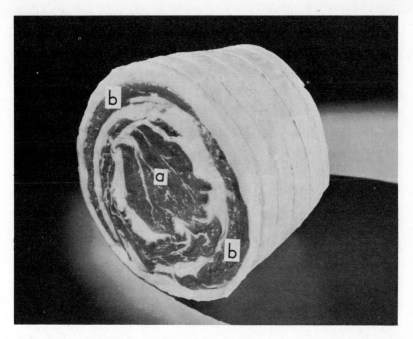

ROLLED RIB

A rolled rib is a standing rib minus the bones. It should be a large enough piece to balance on a rack, fat side up as in the photograph. (a) The rib "eye" muscle. (b) The small outer muscles and the tail of the rib (down to the short-rib section). A properly rolled rib should not contain too much tail, it should not contain the parchmentlike tissue between the ribs (all too often this *is* left in—a meat cutter will simply cut out the ribs one by one instead of slicing all the bone section out at once), and it should be tied so that the string pierces part of the fat and lean each time it goes around the roast. This holds the roast tightly together when shrinkage occurs during the cooking.

Prepare a rolled rib as you would a standing rib. The oven

should be the same temperature and the thermometer readings should be the same, but a rolled roast will require a little longer cooking time: about 32 minutes per pound for a rare roast, 38 minutes per pound for a medium roast, and 48 minutes per pound for a well-done roast. And the time will vary somewhat as before, depending on the size of the roast.

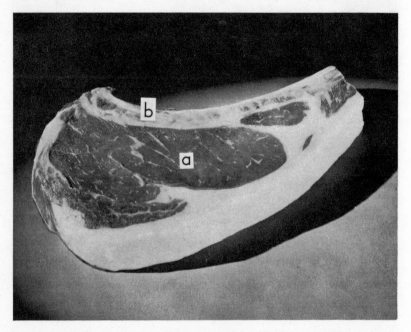

RIB STEAK

A rib steak is a slice from the standing rib. Often it will contain a rib, although it can be cut from between the ribs. (a) The rib eye. (b) A rib. This cut can be broiled or panbroiled. When broiling, count on the same length of time as you would for a club steak.

SHORT RIBS

As you can see on the Beef Cut Chart, short ribs come from the bottom of the rib section and the top of the short plate. They can be cut into cubes, as you see in the photograph; or left in longer strips, each containing a rib; or left in a larger piece that contains several ribs.

Short ribs can be braised or used for stew meat. Braising until tender will take about 2 or 3 hours.

SHORT PLATE—Wholesale Cut

The cut called the short plate is under the rib section. It contains the ends of the ribs. The fat and lean are in layers.

PLATE BEEF

In the photograph the piece has been sliced at the end of the rib section (a) and folded back on itself. The plate is sometimes boned and rolled. You can distinguish it from a rolled rib because it will have no "eye" muscle. Plate beef should be braised or simmered.

CHUCK—Wholesale Cut

If you will look at the Beef Bone Chart, you will see that the chuck is an almost square section cut from the front end of the carcass. It contains the fifth through the first ribs; the bladebone or scapula; part of the arm bone, or humerus; and the neck bone. This section contains many muscles going in various directions. Because the shoulder is a much used section of the animal, it contains a good deal of connective tissue and lean with a somewhat coarser grain than is found in, for instance, the short loin. But meat cut from the shoulder is juicy and very palatable. The more tender meat in the section is found, understandably, closest to the rib section.

There are various ways of cutting the chuck into retail pieces. On the Beef Cut Chart the dotted lines show one way, producing a triangle pot roast and a shoulder filet. A somewhat more common way is to cut more or less straight down from the top of the back to a little past the bladebone. This method produces blade roasts, each containing a portion of the backbone, the bladebone, and the ribs. The arm roast is usually cut as indicated on the chart.

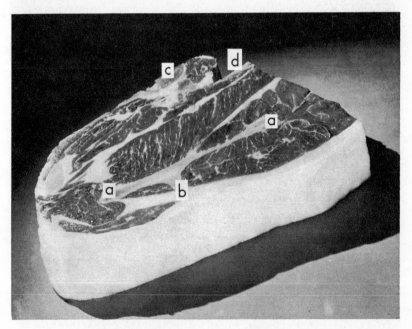

BLADE POT ROAST OR CHUCK ROAST

Blade Pot Roast or Chuck Roast. (See preceding page.) When my food-shopping days first began, I thought a blade roast meant that the piece of meat had been cut with a big knife blade from heaven knows where on the animal. Somehow the idea of an animal having shoulder blades just like mine (almost) did not enter my head. A blade pot roast has as its significant feature a cross section of the bladebone (a). (b) The ridge of the bladebone (you have a ridge too). As you can see on the Beef Bone Chart, the ridge will be closer to the top of the bladebone the nearer the cut is to the front of the animal; around the first ribs, the cross section will resemble a figure 7 and it will be smaller. By looking at the position of the ridge you can tell from where in the chuck the cut has been taken. (c) The backbone. This bone will also indicate from where the cut has been taken; the closer it is to the top of the bladebone, the nearer the cut is to the first ribs. (d) The ribs will be found here. The blade roast containing the fifth and fourth ribs has a lower percentage of lean and a higher percentage of fat and bone than roasts containing the third, second, or first ribs.

Chuck roasts are cut in varying sizes and shapes. All the roasts you see in your meat market may not resemble the one in the photograph. The various cuts have been given different names in many parts of the country; for example, bread-and-butter roast. Ask your meat cutter the origin of the cut if you can't recognize it and are curious. By knowing this, you may be able to determine how much bone the cut will contain.

Thin slices from the blade cut are called blade steaks. A cut from the chuck may be boned and rolled; it is called a boneless chuck.

To cook: These roasts, rolled chucks, and steaks should be braised. The roast may be nicely marinated (see Chapter 7), and the wine and vegetables of the marinade add to the flavor. Sauces—any of the Brown Sauce variations in Chapter 8—served with the roast also enhance the flavor,.and such sauces served with leftover pot roast are a great addition. You should count on about 3 or more hours cooking time, depending on the size of the cut.

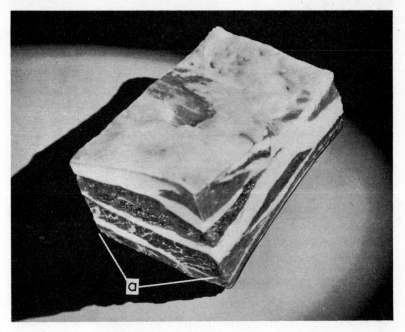

ENGLISH OR BOSTON CUT

The Beef Cut Chart will show you the origin of this cut, from the inner corner of a square-cut chuck. (a) Two or three ribs appear in cross section here. As you can see, this cut contains a considerable portion of fat.

Braising is the method of cooking, and the length of cooking time will be similar to that of the chuck roast.

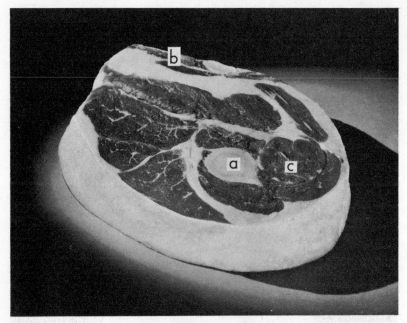

ARM POT ROAST

This cut contains a cross section of the humerus, or arm bone (a), and includes a cross section of three or four ribs (b). Do not confuse this cut with a thick round cut (p. 98) from the hind leg; study the two photographs, and you can easily see a difference in muscle formation. A helpful pointer is the round muscle (c); this tender muscle is completely surrounded by connective tissue. The arm pot roast contains quite a bit of fat but proportionately very little bone.

Thin slices from the arm are called steaks.

The roast and the steaks should be braised in the same manner as a blade pot roast.

BRISKET—*Wholesale Cut*

The brisket contains the lower portions of ribs 5 through 1 and the breastbone. About 50 per cent of the cut is lean, about 35 per cent is fat, and about 15 per cent is bone. The cut has excellent flavor.

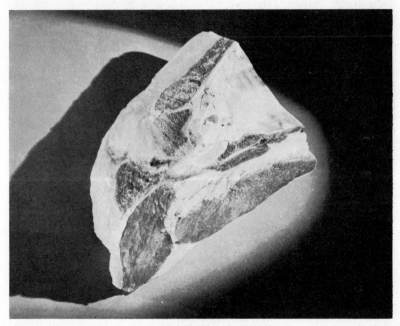

FRESH BRISKET

This cut is composed of layers of lean and fat, and it will contain the breastbone. All or part of the cut can be braised or simmered. Count on about 3 or 4 hours cooking time to tenderize the meat. A well-known way of serving simmered brisket is with a pungent Horseradish Sauce (see Index).

Corned Beef. Corning is a form of curing. The rather odd name derives from the fact that in Europe the pellets of salt rubbed into the meat were the size of kernels of grain, the word corn being used for any type of grain.

A boned brisket is most often used for corning. In the corning process, the beef is held for a certain length of time in a brine solution. When you buy corned beef, you should ask your meat cutter if it should be soaked in water to remove some of the salt—this is sometimes the case unless the meat has been given what is called a mild cure. If soaking is required, allow ten hours for this and change the water four times during the soaking period.

To cook: Corned beef should be simmered about 5 hours in enough water to cover. A few peppercorns, a bay leaf, a pinch of thyme, and a clove of garlic may be added to the water, and vegetables such as carrots, celery, onions, parsley, may be added during the last 45 mintues. Again, Horseradish Sauce gives added flavor, or serve the corned beef with Robert Sauce (see Index).

Ever heard of corned beef and cabbage? Some cooks say to simmer a head of cabbage the entire time with the beef, others say to add it the last 15 minutes or so, and still others say to boil it separately. I prefer the last; there is something not too appealing about greasy cabbage.

FORESHANK—Wholesale Cut

The foreshank contains two bones, the ulna and the radius, just as in the human forearm. It also contains the knuckle, or elbow bone. The proportions of lean to bone in this cut are just about equal; only about 10 per cent of the cut is fat.

Naturally, there is a good amount of connective tissue in the foreshank.

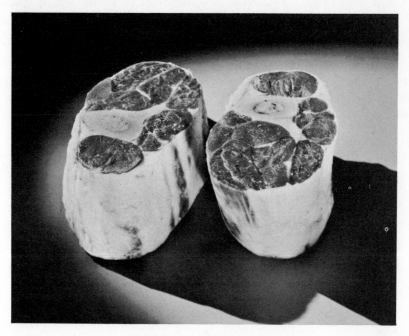

SHANK CROSS CUTS

The photograph is self-explanatory. These cuts may be braised and they make excellent meat for soup.

VARIETY MEATS

This rather vague term covers quite a variety of items:

Oxtail. A beef tail is called an "oxtail." The tail, which weighs 1½ to 2 pounds, obviously contains a lot of bone, but, nevertheless, the cut is good braised or used as meat for soup.

Liver. Beef liver is good for you, but its flavor is rather strong for most palates. Some meat markets have what is called baby-beef liver. This comes from a young steer or heifer and is less strong than liver from a full-grown animal. See liver, in the chapter on veal, for methods of cooking baby-beef liver.

Kidney. Beef and veal kidneys can be distinguished from those of lamb and pork by the lobulations the former have on the surface. A beef kidney usually weighs about one pound.

Beef kidney is best if it is marinated (see Chapter 7) a few hours, or you may soak it in cold water to which a teaspoon or so of lemon juice has been added. The excess fat, capsule, gristle, and tubes should be cut out; this is easier if you first split the kidney lengthwise. It is important to do all this *before* you wash the kidney. Then drain and marinate or soak as described.

Kidneys may be braised, using some of the marinade for the liquid; broiled, if cut into slices ½ inch thick or less (be sure to baste often); or cubed, and made into a stew.

If you object to the strong flavor of beef kidneys, try those from veal or lamb.

Heart. The beef heart is a rather large organ weighing 3 to 4 pounds. It is, naturally, a much used muscle and consequently tends to be tough unless cooked by slow, moist heat. It should be washed well in cold water. The large veins and arteries should be cut off. Marinating helps to tenderize beef heart. Then simmer or braise it for 3 to 5 hours. You may stuff it with a flavorful dressing before cooking (see Index for Beef Heart Braised in Wine).

Brains. A beef brain usually weighs 13 to 14 ounces. Wash the brain well under cold running water and remove the membrane. Simmer for 15 minutes in water to which 1 tablespoon of lemon juice or vinegar, 1 teaspoon of salt, a pinch of thyme, and ½ bay leaf have been added. Drain.

So many people associate nothing with brains (beef brains, that is) except scrambled eggs. For a delicious variation cut the brain into slices after simmering, and dredge the slices with flour or dip in dried bread crumbs seasoned with salt and pepper. Sauté them in lots of butter, and serve with a sauce— German Sauce, Bordelaise Sauce, or Curry Sauce (see Index); or melted butter and minced parsley and/or mushrooms; or lightly browned butter with capers added at the last minute. Serve with wedges of lemon.

Tongue. A most flavorful and economical meat. A beef tongue usually weighs 3 to 4 pounds, and with the exception of the skin and a few roots at the base, it is all edible lean meat. You can buy beef tongues fresh, corned, pickled, or smoked.

Fresh tongue should be simmered for about 3 hours in salted water (½ teaspoon of salt per pound of tongue and water enough to cover) to which have been added a few peppercorns, a large onion stuck with a couple of cloves, a bay leaf, a carrot cut into rounds, a stalk of celery cut into slices, and a branch of parsley. When tender, let the tongue cool in the broth and, when it is cool enough to handle, pull off the skin and cut off the roots.

Serve tongue sliced thin (against the grain), with horseradish, mustard, or a mixture of the two; or with a sauce—Hunter's Sauce, Robert Sauce, Devil Sauce, or Lyonnaise Sauce (see Index).

A corned, smoked, or pickled tongue may be prepared in the same manner. It is wise, however, to soak it in cold water for a few hours before cooking.

Tripe. The muscular lining of the beef stomach. Honeycomb tripe, the most delicate in flavor, is the lining of the second stomach of beef cattle. Tripe is always partially cooked when you buy it, but further simmering of 3 to 5 hours is necessary to tenderize it. Tripe is also sold pickled; this will cook in a shorter period of time.

After tripe has been simmered until tender, it may be cut into strips, brushed generously with melted butter, and broiled (2 to 3 minutes per side); or dipped in fritter batter and deep-fat fried; or dredged with flour, sautéed in butter, and served with Béchamel Sauce (see Index).

GROUND BEEF

No photograph—I'm sure you know what ground beef looks like (maybe all too well!). The meat that is used for ground beef comes from almost anywhere on the animal except the internal organs or glands. A meat cutter who is careful and not wasteful will save all the lean trimmings from meat he has cut and add these to meat from the flank, shank, plate, heel of the round to make up his ground-beef supply. Ideally, ground beef should be about 75 per cent lean and 25 per cent fat, but it seems to be the common practice in meat markets these days to sell two grades of ground beef, the less expensive of the two consisting of what too often looks to be about 65 per cent lean and 35 per cent fat. A good deal of the excess fat, of course, melts away in the cooking; but, on the other hand, fat contributes to the flavor.

If you are curious about how much you actually pay per pound for ground beef after it has been cooked, or if you want to compare the two ground beefs in your market, try this experiment in your kitchen: Purchase an identical weight of the two varieties, enough, for instance, for one patty of each. Cook both patties at the same time in the same pan. Weigh each patty separately after it is cooked (use a postage scale or the like). Subtract each cooked weight from its original raw weight, then divide this difference into the raw weight. This will give you the percentage of loss from each original weight.

Multiply each original cost by its percentage of weight loss. Then add this figure to the original cost. This will give you the actual price you pay for your cooked ground beef. Even if you don't care for arithmetic, this is worth doing, for it will show you which of the two varieties is actually the more economical to buy.

If you grind your own beef, which is really very easy to do, you can regulate the amount of fat to suit yourself.

Beef Recipes

See Chapter 8 for a number of sauces that are good with beef.

ROUND STEAK IN RED WINE

(For 4)

2-lb. round steak, cut thick
1/2 cup flour, about
Salt and pepper
2 tablespoons butter, or 1 tablespoon each butter and olive
  oil
1 carrot, diced
1 large onion, chopped
1 tablespoon chopped parsley
1/2 cup tomato juice
1/2 cup dry red wine

With the back of a heavy knife or the edge of a plate pound the flour, salt, and pepper into the steak. Heat the butter and/or olive oil in a skillet, and in it brown the meat on both sides over rather high heat (about 15 minutes). Add carrot, onion, and parsley. Color the vegetables for 5 minutes, stirring occasionally. Add tomato juice. Cover skillet tightly and simmer over a low heat. When meat has cooked 1 to 1½ hours (depending on its state of tenderness), add the wine. Cook, covered, for another ½ hour, or until the meat is completely tender.

FLEMISH STEAK
(For 4)

2-lb. round steak, cut thick
3 tablespoons butter, lard, or bacon drippings
1 large onion, chopped
1 cup beer
Bouquet garni (1 bay leaf, sprig parsley, ¼ teaspoon dried thyme)
1 cup Brown Sauce (see Index)

Melt 1 tablespoon of the fat in a large skillet, and in it brown the round steak quickly on both side. When brown, remove from the skillet, add the remaining fat to the skillet, and in this lightly sauté the onion. Remove and reserve half of the onion, return the steak to the skillet, and cover it with the reserved onion. Add the beer, the bouquet garni, and the Brown Sauce. Cover and cook in a 275° oven for 2 hours. When the meat is done, place it on a hot platter, skim some of the fat from the sauce, remove the bouquet garni, and reduce the sauce by boiling if it is a little thin. Add salt to taste if necessary. Pour the sauce over the steak and serve.

BEEF STROGANOFF
(For 4)

1½ lbs. top round steak, cut into ⅓- by 2-inch strips
1 large or 2 medium onions, minced
3 tablespoons butter, or 5 tablespoons butter if mushrooms used are fresh
3 tablespoons flour
1 can beef consommé

1 tablespoon catsup
1 teaspoon Worcestershire Sauce
⅛ teaspoon pepper
½ teaspoon dried basil
Dash nutmeg
½ lb. fresh mushrooms, or 6-oz. can mushrooms
1 cup sour cream, warmed to room temperature

In a skillet sauté the onion in 3 tablespoons of butter until pale
yellow. Stir in flour and gradually add the consommé, stirring
constantly. Add catsup, Worcestershire Sauce, pepper, basil, and
nutmeg. Slowly simmer this mixture for at least 15 minutes;
stir occasionally. Meanwhile, in another skillet very lightly
greased with butter and lightly salted, brown the strips of meat.
Cooking time for the meat will depend on tenderness of the
cut. When the meat strips are tender, add them to the sauce.
If you are using fresh mushrooms, melt 2 tablespoons of butter
in the meat skillet and sauté them in it for 5 to 10 minutes. Add
mushrooms to the sauce (if they are canned, add them, drained,
at this time). Taste sauce to see if salt is needed. Just before
serving, stir in the sour cream; heat but do not allow to boil.
Serve with rice and/or slices of dark bread.

BORDELAISE STEAK

(For 4)

1½- to 2-lb. steak, 1 inch thick
Pepper
1 small onion, chopped
1 teaspoon flour
½ cup dry red wine
½ cup beef stock or consommé

Grease a heated skillet with a small amount of suet or butter. Sprinkle steak with pepper. Panbroil to the desired degree of doneness, then remove to a hot platter. Cook the onion in the skillet for 1 to 2 minutes. Stir in the flour and slowly add the wine and stock, stirring constantly. Quickly boil until mixture is thick and dark. Season with salt to taste. Pour sauce over steak on a platter and serve garnished with parsley.

HEADWAITER STEAK

(For 4)

1½- to 2-lb. steak, 1½ to 2 inches thick for broiling
4 to 6 tablespoons butter, softened to room temperature
1 tablespoon minced parsley
¼ teaspoon dry mustard
Lemon juice
Salt and pepper to taste

Broil steak to desired degree of doneness.* Just before serving, spread on top of the steak a thin layer of butter into which the parsley, mustard, lemon juice, and salt and pepper have been blended.

---

* See time tables for broiling steak earlier in this chapter, or in the Appendix.

FILETS MIGNONS BÉARNAISE
(For 4)

4 4- to 6-oz. filets mignons
4 tablespoons butter
4 slices French bread, ½ inch thick
French-fried potatoes

Béarnaise Sauce:

1 tablespoon minced green onion
¼ teaspoon dried tarragon
¼ teaspoon dried chervil
Pinch dried thyme
Small piece bay leaf
3 tablespoons white-wine vinegar
3 tablespoons dry white wine
Pinch each salt and pepper
2 egg yolks, slightly beaten
4 tablespoons butter
Dash cayenne pepper

Béarnaise Sauce: In a saucepan put the onion, tarragon, chervil, thyme, bay leaf, vinegar, wine, salt and pepper. Reduce by boiling to one third of original volume. Allow to cool to lukewarm. Add the egg yolks, which have been diluted with 1 teaspoon of water. With a fork or sauce whisk, beat the mixture over a very low heat, or over hot water, and when it begins to thicken, add the butter little by little. When the sauce is thick, strain through a fine sieve, and stir in the cayenne.

This is an excellent sauce for any broiled steak. Start cooking the steak when the béarnaise is almost done; away from the heat, the sauce can wait.

Broil or sauté the filets, making certain they are well lubricated with butter while cooking.* Meanwhile, sauté the French bread slices in the remaining butter, turning often. When the meat is cooked, place each filet on a slice of bread and arrange these in a circle on a hot platter. On top of each filet, around the edge, spoon a border of the sauce, and fill the center of the platter with French-fried potatoes.

FILETS MIGNONS WITH MUSHROOMS

(For 4)

4 4- to 6-oz. filets mignons
½ lb. fresh mushrooms, or 6-oz. can mushrooms
6 tablespoons butter, about
½ tablespoon flour
¾ cup heavy cream
4 slices French bread, ½ inch thick
⅓ cup dry sherry
Salt and pepper

Sauté fresh mushrooms in 2 to 3 tablespoons of butter for about 5 minutes. If canned mushrooms are used, drain, and merely color them in the butter. Stir in the flour and slowly add the cream. Mix thoroughly and add salt and pepper to taste. Keep this mixture hot but do not allow it to boil.

Sauté the French bread slices until golden brown in a good amount of butter, turning often; keep warm. Sauté the filets in the same skillet, making certain they are well lubricated with

* See time table for broiling filets mignons earlier in this chapter, or in the Appendix.

butter while cooking. Put the meat, when cooked, on the bread and arrange in a circle on a hot platter. Pour the mushroom and cream mixture into the center of the platter. Into the pan in which the filets have cooked stir the sherry, mixing it with any leftover meat juice. Salt and pepper to taste. Bring to a good boil and pour a little of this over each filet.

BRAISED BEEF FILET

(For 4 to 6)

1 whole beef filet or tenderloin
Several lardoons of salt pork
2 tablespoons butter
1 medium onion, sliced
1 carrot, cut in rounds
½ cup Madeira or dry white wine
½ cup Brown Sauce (see Index)
1 teaspoon meat extract

Lard the filet uniformly over the surface with the salt pork (see Chapter 7). Melt the butter in a skillet and in it brown the meat on all sides. When the meat is thoroughly browned, add the onion slices and carrot rounds. Lightly sauté the vegetables, then add the wine, Brown Sauce, and meat extract. Cover the skillet and continue the cooking in a 325° oven; allow about 15 minutes per pound but never longer than 40 minutes *total* cooking time no matter what the weight of the filet. When the meat is done, place it on a hot platter. Strain the sauce from the skillet through a sieve and pour it over the filet.

Garnish with one of the following:

A series of small portions of French-fried or sautéed potatoes, peas, carrots, and green beans. Repeat until you have completely surrounded the filet. Be sure the vegetables are well drained.

A series of small portions of sautéed mushrooms, grilled slices of tomato, and asparagus tips. Repeat until you have completely surrounded the filet.

A roasted filet can also be served with these same garnishes.

BROILED FLANK STEAK

(For 3 or 4)

1 flank steak
1 medium onion, sliced
1 clove garlic, sliced
1/4 cup olive or other salad oil
2 tablespoons soy sauce
5 tablespoons white-wine vinegar
4 peppercorns, crushed
2 tablespoons butter

Have your meat cutter run the steak through the tenderizer once or twice. Remove any connective tissue and fat. Place the steak and all of the above ingredients except the butter in an earthenware or glass bowl and marinate the steak for at least 6 hours, turning it two or three times during marination.

Broil the steak in a hot preheated broiler, 4 inches from the heat, allowing approximately 15 minutes per side. Sauté the onion slices from the marinade in the 2 tablespoons of butter and pour them, with the butter, over the steak when it is done. Carve the steak against the grain. Serve with buttered noodles.

STUFFED FLANK STEAK
(For 3 or 4)

1 flank steak
Salt and pepper
3 tablespoons butter
2 tablespoons chopped onion
4 fresh mushrooms, or 2-oz. can mushrooms, finely chopped
¾ cup bread crumbs
1 egg, slightly beaten
¼ lb. sausage meat
⅛ teaspoon dried thyme
1 cup beef stock
1 tablespoon flour

Have your meat cutter run the steak through the tenderizer once or twice. Remove any connective tissue and fat, and season the steak with salt and pepper.

Prepare the dressing by sautéing the onion and mushrooms in 1 tablespoon of the butter. Remove from the heat and add the bread crumbs, egg, sausage meat, and thyme. Mix thoroughly and add salt and pepper to taste. Spread this dressing over the steak, roll it up like a jelly roll, and tie it securely in several places.

Heat 1 tablespoon butter in a skillet and brown the roll on all sides. Add the beef stock, cover, and continue cooking in a 325° oven for about 1½ hours. When steak is tender, remove to a hot platter. Thicken the liquid remaining in the skillet with 1 tablespoon each of flour and butter that have been kneaded together. Pour the sauce over the steak. Serve sliced; do not remove string until after the slices have been transferred to each plate.

MARINATED POT ROAST

(For 4)

3- to 4-lb. pot roast (round, rump, or chuck)
Several lardoons salt pork
⅛ teaspoon garlic powder, about
Marinade
2 tablespoons rendered beef suet or lard
2 tablespoons flour
1 tablespoon white-wine vinegar

Lard the meat with the lardoons which have first been rolled in the garlic powder. Marinate for at least 12 hours (see Chapter 7).

When the meat is ready to cook, melt the fat in a heavy kettle over high heat. Brown the meat quickly on all sides. When brown, sprinkle meat with flour and add the onion and carrot slices from the marinade to the kettle. Allow the flour and vegetables to color for about 3 minutes. Then add the marinade to the kettle; the liquid should reach half way up the roast. Bring the marinade quickly to a boil and let it continue boiling for 3 to 5 minutes. Baste the top of the roast well with the marinade, cover the kettle, and either reduce the heat to a simmer and continue to cook on top of the stove, or place the kettle in a 325° oven. Cooking time should be from 2 to 3 hours.

When the meat is tender, remove it to a hot platter. Strain the liquid from the kettle into a saucepan and reduce to desired richness by boiling. Taste to see if salt should be added, add 1 tablespoon white-wine vinegar, and serve the sauce in a gravy boat.

CREOLE BEEF

(For 4)

3 to 4 lbs. beef from round, rump, or chunk
Salt and pepper
2 tablespoons olive oil
2 medium onions, sliced
1 tablespoon tomato paste
1 clove garlic
¼ teaspoon dried thyme
Sprig parsley
1 or 2 pinches saffron

Cut the beef into 2-inch cubes, and salt and pepper them. Heat the oil in a large skillet or a heavy kettle. Lay the onion slices flat in the bottom of the skillet, and sauté them for about 2 minutes. Arrange the beef cubes on top of the onions. Then add the tomato paste, garlic, thyme, parsley, and saffron. Cover tightly and simmer for 2 to 3 hours. The ingredients themselves should supply sufficient moisture, but add a little water if the skillet goes dry from escaping moisture.

To serve, remove the garlic and parsley, place the beef cubes in a hot serving dish, and pour the sauce from the skillet over them. Rice goes well with Creole Beef.

GRILLED OXTAIL

(For 4)

2 oxtails, cut into sections
2 tablespoons butter
1 onion, sliced
1 carrot, cut in rounds
2 cups beef stock
¼ teaspoon dried thyme
1 bay leaf
Sprig parsley
½ clove garlic
2 tablespoons butter, melted
1 cup dry bread crumbs, about

Melt 2 tablespoons of butter in a deep kettle. Add onion and carrot slices and allow them to color for about 5 minutes. Add the oxtail sections. Pour in the beef stock and add the thyme, bay leaf, parsley, and garlic. Cover the kettle and simmer for 3 to 5 hours, or until the meat is tender. When the oxtails are thoroughly cooked, let them cool in the broth.

Pour the 2 tablespoons of melted butter into a flat dish and thoroughly douse each oxtail section in it. Then salt and pepper the sections and roll them in the bread crumbs. Broil under medium heat, about 4 inches from the flame, until they are thoroughly heated and golden brown. Serve with either Bordelaise Sauce, Devil Sauce, or Robert Sauce (see Index).

BEEF HEART BRAISED IN WINE

(For 4)

1 beef heart
2 tablespoons white-wine vinegar
¾ lb. sausage meat
1 large onion, chopped
1 4-oz. can chopped mushrooms
1 cup bread crumbs
1 tablespoon chopped parsley
Salt and pepper to taste
3 tablespoons butter
2 tablespoons flour
1 cup dry red wine
1 cup beef bouillon

Wash the heart well under running cold water. Remove veins and arteries. Place the heart in an earthenware or glass bowl and cover with cold water. Add the vinegar and soak overnight in this solution.

Prepare a dressing by lightly browning the sausage meat in a skillet. Remove the meat but let the fat remain. In this fat sauté the onion and mushrooms. Add the vegetables to the sausage, and mix in the bread crumbs, parsley, salt and pepper.

Stuff the heart, which has first been drained and wiped dry, with the dressing and tie it closed. In a heavy kettle melt the butter, and in it brown the heart well on all sides. Sprinkle with the flour, allow flour to color slightly, then add the wine and bouillon. Simmer, covered, until tender (3 to 5 hours).

Serve the heart sliced, with some of the liquid in which it has cooked.

BEEF TONGUE CASSEROLE
(For 4 to 6)

1 fresh beef tongue
1 cup dry white wine
2 tablespoons white-wine vinegar
1 medium onion, chopped
1/4 teaspoon dried thyme
1/2 bay leaf
4 peppercorns, crushed
1 cup Brown Sauce (see Index)
2 teaspoons chopped parsley
Dash cayenne pepper
4 to 5 tablespoons bread crumbs
1 to 2 tablespoons butter

Cook the tongue until tender (see p. 131). When it has cooled in its broth, drain it, remove skin, and slice (across the grain) as thinly is possible.

In a saucepan boil the onion, thyme, bay leaf, and peppercorns in the wine and vinegar until the volume is reduced by one half. Strain the mixture through a sieve. Add the Brown Sauce, parsley, and a good dash of cayenne. Mix thoroughly.

In a buttered casserole arrange the slices of tongue in layers, covering each layer with some of the sauce. Sprinkle the bread crumbs over the top and dot with the butter. Bake in a 350° oven for about 30 minutes, or until the bread crumbs are nicely browned.

GERMAN BEEFSTEAK
(For 4)

1 to 1½ lbs. lean ground beef
1 onion, chopped
4 tablespoons butter
2 eggs
2 to 3 slices white bread
1 teaspoon salt
Pepper to taste
Dash nutmeg

Put the ground beef in a large bowl. Sauté the onion lightly in 1 to 2 tablespoons of butter, and add both onion and butter to the beef. Break eggs onto the beef, and add the bread slices, which have first been soaked for a couple of minutes in cold water and then squeezed nearly dry. Add the seasonings. With your hands thoroughly blend all these ingredients. Form into four patties and dredge them with flour. Melt the 2 to 3 remaining tablespoons of butter in a skillet. Over fairly high heat brown the patties well on both sides. Lower the heat a little and continue cooking until the patties are only moderately rare in the center.

Serve the patties with a sprinkling of lightly sautéed onion on top, or with Robert Sauce or Basic Brown Sauce (see Index).

RUSSIAN BEEFSTEAK
(For 4)

1 to 1½ lbs. very lean ground beef
¼ lb. butter, warmed to room temperature
1 teaspoon salt
Pepper to taste
Dash nutmeg
Flour
½ cup sour cream
¼ cup beef consommé
1 onion, chopped and browned until crisp in butter

Mix together thoroughly the ground beef, 5 tablespoons of the butter, and the salt, pepper, and nutmeg. Form patties and dredge them with flour. In a skillet melt the remaining 3 tablespoons of butter and in it brown the patties well. When the meat is done (cooking time should be 15 to 20 minutes), remove it from the skillet to a hot platter. Into the juices remaining in the skillet stir the sour cream and consommé. The sauce should be hot but it should not be allowed to boil. Pour this over the patties and put on top of each patty a spoonful of crisply browned onion.

BEEF FRICADELLES

(For 4)

1 to 1½ lbs. leftover roast beef, ground
2 medium potatoes
Beef consommé
2 large onion, minced
4 tablespoons butter
1 egg
Salt and pepper to taste
Dash nutmeg

Prepare rather dry mashed potatoes, using a small amount of beef consommé instead of milk to moisten them. Sauté the onion in 2 tablespoons of the butter. In a large bowl, with your hands, blend all the ingredients together thoroughly. Shape into patties and brown in the remaining 2 tablespoons of butter. When the patties are well browned, lower the heat and cook a little longer, until they are well heated through.

Serve with Robert Sauce or Basic Brown Sauce (see Index).

CHAPTER 11

VEAL

Veal is the meat from calves of either sex. The best veal comes usually from milk-fed animals between six to ten weeks of age and weighing about 150 pounds. The young of beef cattle are divided into two groups: vealers—usually not over three months of age and weighing from 110 to 180 pounds; and calves—from three to nine months of age and weighing up to 300 pounds. After a certain age, a calf has been fed, entirely or in part, on feed other than milk.

✿ Veal of Good Quality: What to Look for

The color of the lean should be a greyish-pink. The more mature the animal and the more it has subsisted on feed other than milk, the more red the lean will be. The lean should be fairly firm; it should have a very fine grain, and it should look velvety. Because veal comes from a young animal, it will have much less finish—that is, distribution of fat—than beef. What exterior fat there is should be white and firm. Veal has little or no marbling.

VEAL BONE CHART

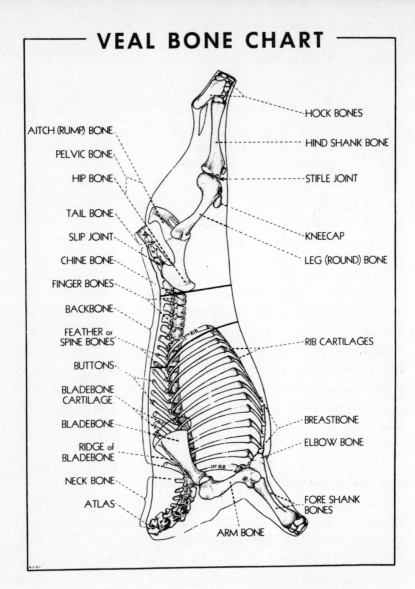

HOCK BONES

HIND SHANK BONE

STIFLE JOINT

KNEECAP

LEG (ROUND) BONE

AITCH (RUMP) BONE

PELVIC BONE

HIP BONE

TAIL BONE

SLIP JOINT

CHINE BONE

FINGER BONES

BACKBONE

FEATHER or
SPINE BONES

BUTTONS

BLADEBONE
CARTILAGE

BLADEBONE

RIDGE of
BLADEBONE

NECK BONE

ATLAS

RIB CARTILAGES

BREASTBONE

ELBOW BONE

FORE SHANK
BONES

ARM BONE

NATIONAL LIVE STOCK AND MEAT BOARD

🏵 How Veal Is Cut

The size of the animal in large part determines how it is to be cut for wholesale distribution. A small vealer may be split in half crosswise, the space between the twelfth and thirteenth ribs being the dividing line. Cutting it in this fashion yields what are called a hindsaddle and a foresaddle. Or the carcass may be split in half lengthwise into sides, in the same manner as beef. Further wholesale and retail cutting of veal is very similar to that of beef; the cuts are simply smaller than those of beef. Or, cuts are combined to yield more pieces large enough for roasts. Refer to the Veal Cut Chart on p. 155 which will help you to follow the descriptions of cuts in this chapter; they are often compared with cuts you will find on the Beef Cut Chart, p. 95. The Veal Bone Chart on p. 152 will locate for you the bones that are mentioned.

🏵 The Cooking of Veal

Veal is usually cooked quite differently from beef. It is tender because it comes from a young animal, but because it lacks fat and has a good amount of connective tissue, it usually requires long, slow cooking. It has a delicate flavor that should be enhanced by the right cooking methods and the use of flavorful sauces. To be properly tender, veal should always be cooked to a fairly well-done stage.

HINDQUARTER OR HINDSADDLE

LEG or ROUND—Wholesale Cut

This cut includes everything from the hock bones up through the hipbone—the shank, the round, and the rump. The bones and muscles, naturally, are very similar to those of beef.

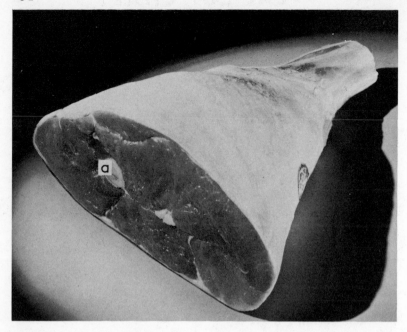

SHANK HALF OF THE LEG

This is the lower half of the leg, minus the hock and the end of the shank bone. It makes a rather large roast. Included in this cut are potential smaller cuts: the heel of the round and the hind shank bone (which includes the shank knucklebone). (a) The round bone.

Braise this cut, about 1½ to 2 hours (see Index for Braised Veal Roast), or roast it. Because of the lack of marbling, it is a great help to lard veal.

To roast: Season the meat, insert a meat thermometer (so it does not rest on bone or fat), and cook on a rack in an uncovered roasting pan. Have the oven preheated to 325°. Roasting time will be about 25 to 30 minutes per pound, and the thermometer

VEAL CUT CHART

Retail Cuts

Wholesale Cuts

Retail Cuts

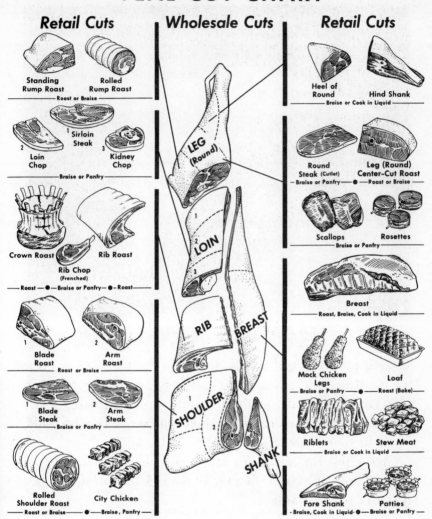

Standing Rump Roast   **Rolled Rump Roast**
— Roast or Braise —

Loin Chop (2)   **Sirloin Steak** (1)   **Kidney Chop** (3)
— Braise or Panfry —

Crown Roast   **Rib Roast**
Rib Chop (Frenched)
— Roast — ● — Braise or Panfry — ● — Roast —

Blade Roast (1)   **Arm Roast** (2)
— Roast or Braise —

Blade Steak (1)   **Arm Steak** (2)
— Braise or Panfry —

Rolled Shoulder Roast   **City Chicken**
— Roast or Braise — ● — Braise, Panfry —

LEG (Round)

LOIN

RIB

SHOULDER

BREAST

SHANK

Heel of Round   **Hind Shank**
— Braise or Cook in Liquid —

Round Steak (Cutlet)   **Leg (Round) Center-Cut Roast**
— Braise or Panfry — ● — Roast or Braise —

Scallops   **Rosettes**
— Braise or Panfry —

Breast
— Roast, Braise, Cook in Liquid —

Mock Chicken Legs   **Loaf**
— Braise or Panfry — ● — Roast (Bake) —

Riblets   **Stew Meat**
— Braise or Cook in Liquid —

Fore Shank   **Patties**
— Braise, Cook in Liquid — ● — Braise or Panfry —

NATIONAL LIVE STOCK AND MEAT BOARD

should register 170° when the meat is done. Baste the roast every half hour with melted butter.

Sour cream, or sweet cream with a dash of lemon juice added, mixed with the juices in the pan makes a nice accompaniment for the roast. Pass this sauce separately.

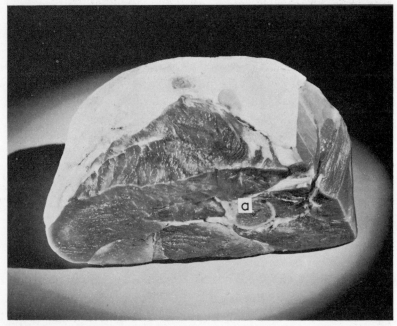

CENTER CUT OF THE LEG

This cut may be bought in various sizes. It will contain almost all of the round bone, when it is a large roast, or only a portion of the round bone. In any case, the proportion of bone to lean is much less than in the shank half of the leg, which allows easier carving. (a) The round bone.

This cut may be braised or roasted in the same manner as the shank half of the leg.

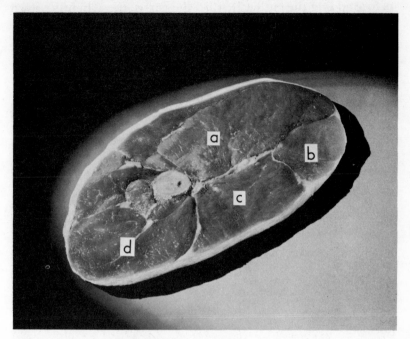

CUTLET OR ROUND STEAK

A veal cutlet is the same cut as a whole beef round steak (p. 98). (a) The top of the round. (b) The "eye" of the round. (c) The bottom of the round. (d) The tip of the round.

Cutlets over an inch thick should be braised. Thinner cuts may also be sautéed. Cookbooks, especially those devoted to European cooking, abound in sauces to make these (and veal scallops) most delicious. See the veal recipes at the end of this chapter for a few examples and also Chapter 8 on sauces.

To braise: Season with salt and pepper and dredge with flour. Melt at least 2 to 3 tablespoons of butter or olive oil in a skillet. You may stir part of a clove of garlic in this for 2 or 3 minutes before adding the cutlet. Discard the garlic, then slightly brown the meat on both sides. Add enough Veal Stock (see Index) or water to cover well the bottom of the skillet, put a lid on the skillet, and cook the cutlet over low heat until tender. This should take 45 minutes to an hour. Remove the cutlet and make a sauce—Sunrise, Hungarian, Portuguese (see Index)—in the liquid remaining in the skillet, and pour it over the cutlet. Or sweet or sour cream alone may be added to the liquid.

To sauté: Bread the cutlet by dredging it with seasoned flour, then dip it in beaten egg and in dry bread crumbs. For a variation, add Hungarian paprika to the flour and 3 to 4 table-spoons of grated Parmesan cheese to the bread crumbs. Heat at least 4 tablespoons of butter or olive oil in a skillet and brown the cutlet in this. Cover the skillet, reduce the heat, and cook slowly until tender; or continue the cooking, pan uncovered, in a 325° oven. Cooking time after browning will be 30 to 45 minutes.

Standing Rump Roast. This cut contains a great deal of bone: the aitchbone, the tail bone, the knuckle where the round bone joins the pelvis, and sometimes part of the round bone. (a) The top of the round. (b) The "eye" of the round. (c) The bottom of the round. (d) The tip of the round. (e) The round bone. It's not much fun trying to carve it! Braise or roast it as you would a leg cut, above.

A much more practical way to buy this cut is in the boneless, rolled state. A rolled veal rump resembles a rolled beef rump (p. 104) except in size, the veal cut being about one third to one half the size. A rolled roast will take 10 to 15 minutes more cooking time per pound than a leg or a standing rump of veal,

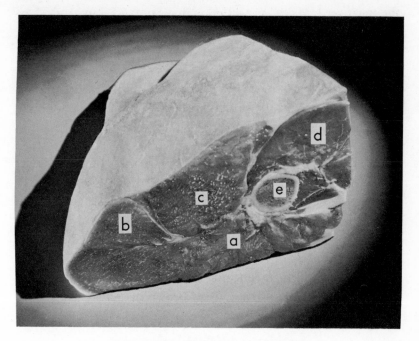

STANDING RUMP ROAST

or about 40 to 45 minutes per pound. The thermometer reading should be 170°.

Occasionally the upper half of the leg and the rump will be cut in one piece. This cut is called the rump half of the leg, as opposed to the shank half of the leg.

Hind Shank. This cut contains part or all of the shank bone, a fair amount of lean, and a great amount of connective tissue. Like the foreshank (p. 174), it is rich in gelatinous substances and can be used in place of the foreshank to make broth (Veal Stock, see Index).

Scallops. A veal scallop is a small boneless cut, usually from the leg, which is pounded very thin. The Italians call such a cut *scaloppine di vitello,* which has been adapted in this country to "veal scallopini." If your market does not have veal scallops, you may make them yourself by pounding a thin veal cutlet with a mallet until it is very thin and then cutting from this round or oval pieces about 4 inches in diameter.

Veal scallops should be breaded or dredged with flour and browned very quickly in hot butter. Some sort of a sauce is a necessity—it may be Sunrise, Hungarian, Portuguese, Mushroom, Hunter's (see Index)—or you can simply add 3 to 4 tablespoons of consommé and about 3 tablespoons of sherry or Marsala to the juices in the pan. Or just add the consommé, and garnish the scallops with several unpeeled slices of lemon, sliced so thin you could read through them; the lemon is eaten rind and all. Sprinkle with chopped parsley.

LOIN—Wholesale Cut

The loin cut of veal corresponds to the combined sirloin and short loin of beef (see Veal and Beef Cut Charts). It may also include the kidney, which often is cut with a roast or chops. Roasts and/or chops are cut from the loin section.

Sirloin Roast. Corresponds to the entire beef sirloin section. Contains the backbone and hipbone and is somewhat difficult to carve because of the proportion and position of these bones. Braise (see Index for Braised Veal Roast) or roast this cut. Roasting time will be about 30 to 35 minutes per pound and the oven temperature should be 325°. Thermometer temperature should reach 170°.

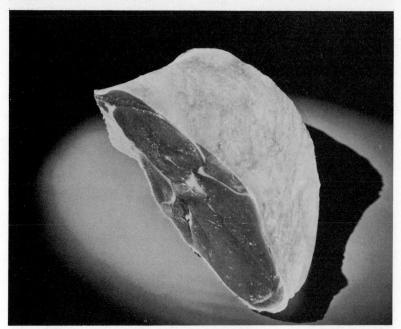

SIRLOIN ROAST

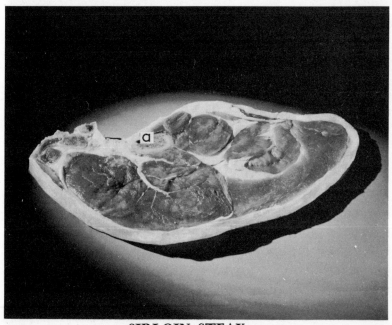

SIRLOIN STEAK

Sirloin Steak. The photograph (see preceding page) is of a round-bone (a) sirloin steak. These veal steaks will closely resemble the same steaks in beef (p. 106). They can be braised or sautéed in the same manner as the cutlet.

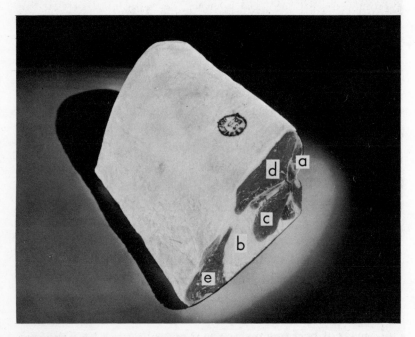

LOIN ROAST

A whole loin roast corresponds to the short loin section of beef. (a) The backbone. (b) The suet. (c) The tenderloin muscle. (d) The loin "eye" muscle. (e) The flank muscle (the "tail"). Roast or braise. The cooking time will be similar to that of a sirloin roast.

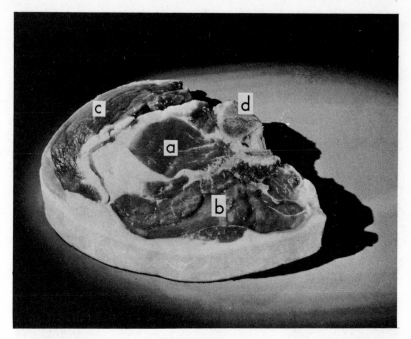

LOIN CHOP

The loin can be cut into chops. A chop, by the way, is a cut of meat that is produced by chopping it through bone from a larger cut with a cleaver, whereas a cutlet is cut with a knife. The loin chops will correspond to porterhouse, T-bone, and club steaks of beef (see pp. 109-111) according to where they are cut. The chop in the photograph would be comparable to a beef porterhouse steak. (a) The tenderloin muscle. (b) The loin "eye" muscle. (c) The "tail." (d) The backbone. Loin chops are supposedly the best veal chops and they will usually cost more than chops from other cuts.

Braise or sauté loin chops as you would a cutlet.

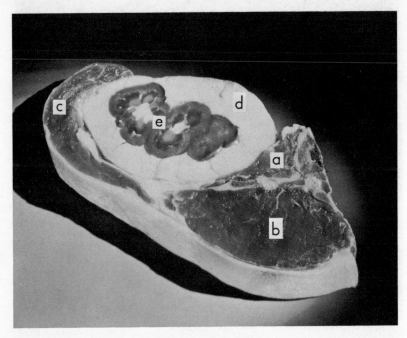

KIDNEY CHOP

A chop from the loin near the rib end. It contains a cross section of the kidney surrounded by a thick layer of fat. (a) A small tenderloin muscle. (b) The loin "eye" muscle. (c) The "tail." (d) Kidney fat. (e) The kidney.

If you like veal kidneys, you will like a veal kidney chop. The good flavor is due to the combination of the lean, fat, and kidney. This chop can be nicely enhanced by one of the Brown Sauces (see Index):

Cook a kidney chop as you would any chop or cutlet, by braising or sautéing.

FOREQUARTER OR FORESADDLE

RIB—Wholesale Cut

This cut corresponds to the rib section of beef (see Veal and Beef Cut Charts). Seven ribs are included.

RIB ROAST

Similar to a standing beef rib roast (p. 117). (a) The rib "eye" muscle. A cut called the hotel rack is the entire rib section of the forequarter—both sides, unsplit. Two rib roasts may also be made into a crown roast (see Veal Cut Chart): the rib ends are

Frenched (all lean and fat cut off, leaving the bone exposed for an inch or so), and the sections are curved back to back and sewed together. This is an eye-catching way to serve a large roast. Stuffing or vegetables may be put in the center.

To roast: Count on 30 to 35 minutes per pound for a standing rib or crown and about 40 to 45 minutes per pound for a rolled roast. The thermometer will read 170° when the roast is done.

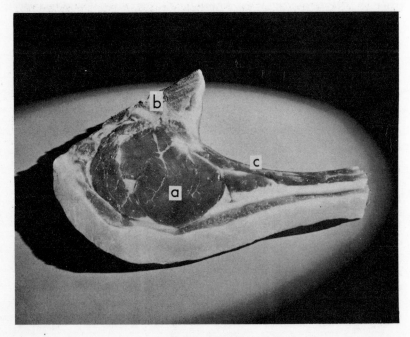

RIB CHOP

A rib chop corresponds to a beef rib steak (p. 120). (a) The rib "eye" muscle. (b) The backbone. (c) The rib. A chop cut between the ribs naturally will have no rib bone. Sauté or braise these chops as you would a cutlet or loin chop.

SHOULDER—*Wholesale Cut*

The shoulder of veal corresponds to the beef chuck (see Veal and Beef Cut Charts). The retail roast cuts are not as many as in beef though often more thin slices (steaks) are cut from the blade and arm regions.

BLADE ROAST

This is cut from the section containing the scapula, or blade-bone. The face of the roast in the photograph is at the forward end of the cut. You may ask your meat cutter to remove the bladebone, leaving a pocket for stuffing. Stuff the pocket with about 2 cups of flavorful stuffing (see Index) and close the opening by tying string tightly around the roast.

Braise (see Index for Braised Veal Roast) or roast a shoulder. Count on about 1½ to 2 hours braising time (nearer 2 hours if the shoulder has been stuffed). A whole shoulder will take about 25 minutes per pound to roast, or 30 to 35 minutes per pound if it is stuffed.

ROLLED SHOULDER

The shoulder in the photograph has been boned and rolled. The string should be tight enough to pierce the fat and a little lean along one side of the section so that the roll will remain compact while it is cooking. Braise like blade roast above, or roast. Roasting time will be about 40 to 45 minutes per pound and braising time 1½ to 2 hours. Oven temperature for roasting should be 325° and the thermometer should read 170° when the roast is done.

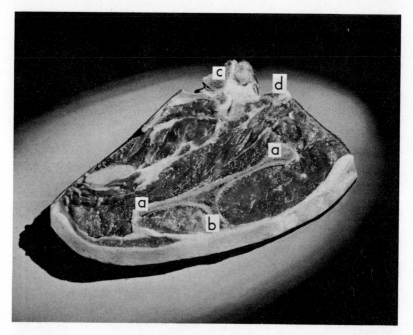

BLADE STEAK

This is cut from the section containing the scapula and it will contain a cross section of this bone (a), with the ridge (b) making the bladebone look like a figure 7 if the cut comes from the foremost part of the section. (c) The backbone, and (d) a rib, unless the slice is made between the ribs. As in beef, a steak from the blade section has muscles going in different directions and it will contain a good deal of connective tissue. These factors, plus the amount of bone present, make the blade steak less expensive than other chops and the cutlet, but it may be cooked in the same manner, either braised or sautéed.

ARM ROAST

This cut is similar to a beef arm pot roast (p. 126). It contains the arm bone (a) and cross sections of from three to five ribs (b)—the first through the fifth ribs. Cooking methods and times are the same as for the veal blade roast.

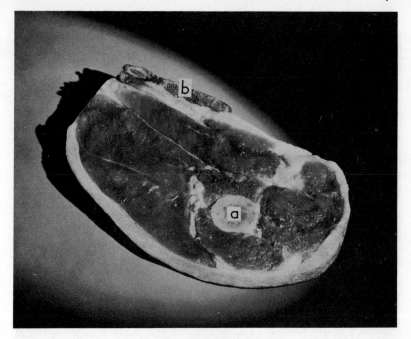

ARM STEAK

Slices from the arm roast cut. As in beef, do not confuse the arm steak with the cutlet from the hind leg. (a) The arm bone. (b) Cross sections of the first ribs. This cut may be braised or sautéed in the same manner as a cutlet, p. 157.

BREAST—Wholesale Cut

This cut includes what would be the brisket, plate, and flank of beef (see Veal and Beef Cut Charts). It contains the rib ends and the breastbone.

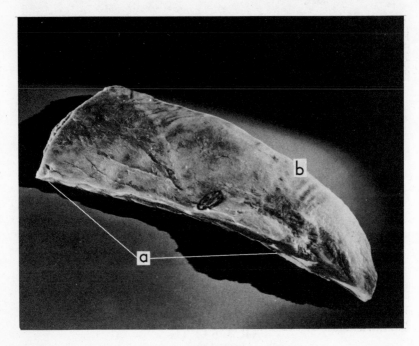

BREAST

The wholesale cut minus the flank end. (a) The rib ends. (b) You will find the breastbone here. Your meat cutter can cut a pocket in the breast between the ribs and the lean. This should be filled with about 3 cups of a flavorful stuffing (see Index), as in a blade roast, and then the opening should be tied or sewed together.

The breast may be also boned and rolled.

If you braise this cut (see Index for Braised Veal Roast), the cooking time will be 1½ to 2 hours. If you roast it, you should allow 40 to 45 minutes per pound and the thermometer should read 170° when the meat is done.

RIBLETS

After the breastbone is removed, cuts are made between the ribs and these riblets are formed. As with beef short ribs, veal riblets can be braised or used for stew meat.

SHANK—Wholesale Cut

The foreshank bones and the knuckle are included in the shank. There is a great deal of connective tissue in this cut and varying amounts of lean.

FORESHANK

Actually, the wholesale cut and the retail cut are usually the same, unless you buy just part of the shank. The gelatin-forming substances in this cut are present in a very high amount, which makes it excellent for making white stock (see Veal Stock in the Index).

VARIETY MEATS

The so-called variety meats of the vealer or calf are considered, for the most part, to be the choicest of any of the animals. The organs are smaller than those of beef and have a more delicate flavor.

Liver. Calf's liver is generally sliced into pieces from ¼ to ¾ of an inch thick. Because of the tenderness of calf's liver and its delicate flavor, the main object in cooking it is to brown the exterior attractively and slightly solidify the interior. In other words, this liver should be pink in the center after it is cooked. Any resemblance a slice of calf's liver has to the old leather sole of a shoe is entirely your fault in cooking—you have cooked it too long!

Calf's liver can be sautéed or broiled. If you plan to sauté it, try to get slices that are consistently of the same thickness, preferably either ¼ or ⅓ of an inch thick. The liver will tend to curl less in cooking if you remove the capsule, or thin outer membrane (some meat markets do this before the liver is put in the display case). Liver should be sautéed very quickly in a little hot butter, bacon drippings, or olive oil. You may season and dredge the slices with flour before cooking. Cooking time will be from about 1 to 3 minutes per side, depending on the thickness.

If you plan to broil the liver, you may have it cut a bit thicker—up to ¾ of an inch. Again, it helps in the cooking if the capsule has been removed. Broil 3 inches from moderate heat for about 2 to 3 minutes on each side, depending on the thickness of the slices. The liver should be oiled or buttered well before broiling because of its complete lack of fat. Season it also before broiling if you wish.

Liver and onions or liver and bacon are well known combinations, but they can become boring. Try serving liver, either sautéed or broiled, with Devil Sauce, Bordelaise Sauce (see Index), or with a tiny bit of minced garlic, parsley, and melted butter on top of each slice. You may also deglaze the pan in which the liver cooked with a little wine vinegar and then add the seasonings and butter.

Kidney. The veal kidney is lobulated as is the beef kidney. Veal kidney has a less strong flavor and is more tender than beef kidney. It can be broiled or sautéed.

To broil, remove the capsule and white core, rinse well, and cut crosswise into ½-inch slices. Saturate the slices with melted butter, salt and pepper them, and broil quickly 3 inches from fairly high heat. Time will be about 5 minutes for each side.

To sauté, prepare as above and cut crosswise into ⅓- to ½-inch slices. Season and sauté quickly in hot butter. Browning time should be about 2 to 3 minutes per side. If you want a well-done slice of kidney, after the initial browning reduce the heat and cook another 5 minutes.

Many sauces enhance kidneys—Bordelaise, Hunter's (with a good supply of mushrooms), Mushroom, or Tarragon (see Index). Or the simple addition of sautéed mushrooms to the kidneys makes a nice variation.

Heart. Two veal hearts equal one beef heart. The veal heart is a little more tender than the beef heart but preparation and cooking methods are the same (see beef heart, p. 130). Cooking times, however, are somewhat less—count on 2½ to 3 hours to simmer or braise a whole veal heart.

Brains. The veal brain is not too much smaller than a beef brain. Prepare and cook in the same manner as beef brain. Cooking times are the same.

Sweetbreads. Sweetbreads are the thymus (a lymphoid organ divided into two parts, or lobes, and found near the heart and throat). The thymus is only present in young animals (including children), but the function of it has as yet not been determined. Beef sweetbreads come from young cattle and are slightly larger than those from veal.

Sweetbreads should be prepared for cooking by first soaking them in cold water for 30 to 45 minutes. The water should be changed three times, or you can soak them under slowly running water. They should be then placed in cold salted water to cover. Bring the water to a boil and boil for 5 minutes. Pour this water off and rinse the sweetbreads under cold running water for about 3 minutes. Remove any thick tissue, blood vessels, or excess fat. Wrap the sweetbreads in a cotton towel and put a heavy weight (an iron skillet, etc.) on top of them. This will press out the excess moisture and break down tough fibers. Allow 30 minutes for this.

Sweetbreads may then be sliced and broiled (3 to 5 minutes per side). Be sure to saturate them first with butter. They may also be sliced, dredged with flour, and sautéed in butter; or larded and braised (see Index for Sweetbreads in Parisian Sauce). Serve them with any of the White Sauce and some of the Brown Sauce variations, for example, Devil Sauce (see Index).

Tongue. A veal tongue is smaller than a beef tongue. See beef tongue, p. 131, for preparation, cooking, and cooking times, although, if the tongue is quite small, count on only 2 to 3 hours of simmering.

GROUND VEAL

As with ground beef, ground veal comes from almost anywhere on the animal except the internal organs and glands. For the most part it is composed of lean and fat from the flank, breast, shank, and neck. Ground veal is usually added to other meats to make meat loaves because its flavor is too subtle for solo use. Finely ground, it is used in "forcemeats," an item of elaborate cuisine of which the stuffing on p. 187 is a simplified example.

Veal Recipes

See Chapter 8 for a number of sauces that are good with veal.

EAST INDIAN VEAL CUTLET

(For 4)

1½- to 2-lb. veal cutlet
Salt and pepper
Flour
3 tablespoons butter
2 tablespoons minced onion
2 teaspoons curry powder
¼ cup dry white wine
½ cup thick cream
Lemon juice

Salt and pepper the cutlet and dredge it with flour. Heat the butter in a large skillet and brown the meat in it on both sides. Then add the onion and sprinkle the curry powder over all. Cover the skillet and simmer the cutlet until tender (30 to 45 minutes). When the meat is cooked, remove it to a hot platter, and stir the wine and cream into the skillet. Heat thoroughly, but do not allow to boil. Give the sauce a good squeeze of lemon juice, pour it over the cutlet, and serve.

VEAL CUTLET PARMIGIANA
(For 4)

1½-lb. veal cutlet
Salt and pepper
Flour
½ teaspoon paprika
3 tablespoons grated Parmesan cheese
1 cup bread crumbs
2 eggs
2 tablespoons butter
2 tablespoons olive oil
½ lb. Mozzarella cheese, sliced thin

Sauce:

3 tablespoons olive oil
2 medium onions, chopped
1 clove garlic, chopped
¼ to ½ teaspoon dried basil
1 No. 2½ (1 lb. 12 oz.) can Italian tomatoes
½ teaspoon sugar
Salt and pepper

Remove bone and fat from the cutlet and divide it into four equal pieces. Salt and pepper the meat and dredge it with flour to which the paprika has been added. Mix the Parmesan cheese and bread crumbs together. Beat the eggs. Dip the floured meat first into the eggs, then into the bread-crumb mixture, making sure they are thoroughly coated. Keep the breaded meat in the refrigerator for at least an hour before cooking.

Make the sauce; see below.

In a skillet heat the butter and olive oil and in it slowly brown the breaded veal. This should take about 15 to 20 minutes. Place the browned meat in a large baking dish or in individual baking dishes. Pour the tomato sauce over them. Place the Mozzarella cheese slices over this. Bake in a 350° oven for 15 to 20 minutes, or until the cheese is melted and streaked with light brown.

Tomato Sauce: Heat the oil in a skillet and in it sauté the onions and garlic until they are pale yellow. Add the basil. Force the tomatoes through a sieve into the skillet. Simmer this mixture for 45 minutes, stirring frequently. Add sugar and salt and pepper to taste. Simmer for 15 minutes more.

VEAL SCALLOPS HUNTER'S STYLE

(For 4)

1½ lbs. veal round, pounded thin and cut into 4-inch pieces
Salt and pepper
4 tablespoons butter
½ lb. fresh mushrooms, or 6-oz. can mushrooms, sliced
3 to 4 green onions, minced
½ cup dry white wine
1 heaping tablespoon tomato paste
¼ cup beef consommé
Chopped parsley

Season the scallops with salt and pepper, and sauté them in the butter until they are golden and tender (from 10 to 15 minutes). Remove them to a hot platter and in the same butter sauté the mushroom slices. When the mushrooms are nicely colored, add the onions. Stir onions and mushrooms together for about 2 minutes, then add the wine. Bring this to a boil and reduce liquid by one half. Add the tomato paste and consommé and blend well. Pour this over the scallops and sprinkle each scallop with chopped parsley.

VEAL SCALLOPS WITH ROSEMARY
(For 4)

1½ lbs. veal round, pounded thin and cut into 4-inch pieces
Salt and pepper
Flour
3 tablespoons butter
½ cup dry white wine
¼ teaspoon dried rosemary

Salt and pepper the scallops and dredge them with flour. Melt the butter in a large skillet and, when the pan is hot (but *not* smoking), brown the scallops. When they are golden brown, add the wine and rosemary. Cover the skillet and cook over low heat for 15 to 20 minutes. Pour the juices from the skillet over the scallops before serving.

PORTUGUESE VEAL CHOPS
(For 4)

4 veal chops, about 1 inch thick
3 tablespoons olive oil
½ cup dry white wine
½ clove garlic, chopped
1 tablespoon chopped parsley

Sauce:

3 fresh tomatoes, peeled, seeded, and chopped
1 onion, minced
¼ clove garlic, grated or pressed
1 tablespoon olive oil
1 tablespoon butter
Salt and pepper

Prepare the sauce first by sautéing the tomatoes, onion, and garlic together in the olive oil and butter. When the mixture thickens (20 to 30 minutes), season to taste with salt and pepper.

In a large skillet sauté the veal chops in olive oil. When they are golden brown, cover the skillet and reduce the heat to a simmer. Cooking time will be about 40 minutes. When the chops are tender, transfer them to a hot platter. To the juices remaining in the skillet add the tomato sauce and white wine. Add the garlic and parsley. Cook for about 3 minutes, stirring constantly, then pour mixture over chops and serve.

VEAL CHOPS WITH GREEN PEPPERS

(For 4)

4 veal chops, about 1 inch thick
Salt and pepper
Flour
2 eggs, beaten
1 cup bread crumbs
5 tablespoons olive oil or butter, in all
2 cloves garlic, sliced
2 large or 3 small green peppers, sliced thin
Lemon juice

Season the chops with salt and pepper and dredge them with flour. Dip them in the beaten eggs and then in the bread crumbs. Heat 3 tablespoons of the olive oil or butter in a large skillet. Sauté the garlic slices in this. When the garlic is soft, push it to one side and brown the breaded chops in the oil. When they are golden brown, finish the cooking, uncovered, in a 325° oven for about 30 minutes or until the chops are tender.

In another skillet heat 2 tablespoons of olive oil or butter and in it sauté the green-pepper slices. This will take about 15 minutes. The skillet can be covered to soften the slices a bit. Add salt and pepper to taste.

When the chops are cooked, remove them to a hot platter and smother them with the sautéed green peppers. Into the skillet in which the chops have cooked squeeze the juice of ½ lemon. Mix and then pour over the chops and peppers.

ROAST VEAL WITH SOUR CREAM
(For 4)

4-lb. veal roast, preferably leg, rib, or loin
1 clove garlic
Salt and pepper
Sprinkle powdered ginger
2 teaspoons tomato paste
4 tablespoons melted butter
½ cup tomato juice
1 cup sour cream

Insert small slips of garlic into the roast at intervals. Season with salt, pepper, and a sprinkle of powdered ginger. Rub this into the meat with your hand. Place the meat in a roasting pan and spread it with the tomato paste. Pour the melted butter over the tomato paste. Roast in a 325° oven. After 30 minutes add the tomato juice. Cooking time will be about 2 hours; the meat thermometer should register 170°. Baste the roast two or three times during the cooking period with the liquid in the pan. Fifteen minutes before meat is to be served, skim off most of the fat from the pan juices and stir in the sour cream. Serve the roast on a hot platter and pass the sour-cream sauce separately.

BRAISED VEAL ROAST

(For 4)

4-lb. veal roast—leg, boned shoulder, rib, loin, or sirloin
Several lardoons salt pork
Salt and pepper
3 tablespoons butter
1 carrot, cut in rounds
1 onion, sliced
1½ cups beef bouillon
Bouquet garni (bay leaf, sprig of parsley, ¼ teaspoon dried
    thyme)

Lard the roast with the salt pork. Rub about 1 teaspoon of salt
and any desired amount of pepper into the surface of the meat.
In a roasting pan or Dutch oven melt the butter. Add the carrot
rounds, onion slices, and then the roast. Baste the meat and
vegetables well with the butter, and then put the pan, uncovered, in a 425° oven. Brown the roast, turning it once or
twice, for about 25 minutes. Then add 1 cup of the bouillon and
allow liquid to reduce to one half its original volume. Now add
the remaining ½ cup of bouillon and the bouquet garni. Cover
the pan tightly, reduce oven temperature to 325°, and continue
the cooking for 1 to 1½ hours. When the roast is tender, move
the pan to medium heat on the top of the stove. Cook, uncovered, for 15 minutes, basting often. Place the roast on a hot
platter and strain the liquid remaining in the pan over it.

BLANQUETTE OF VEAL

(For 4)

2 lbs. veal breast or shoulder, cut for stewing
5 tablespoons butter, in all
2 carrots, cut in halves
1 large onion, quartered
1 teaspoon salt
1 tablespoon flour
Hot water
Bouquet garni (bay leaf, sprig of parsley, ¼ teaspoon dried
   thyme, plus 1 clove)
½ clove garlic
12 small white onions
½ lb. fresh mushrooms, or 6-oz. can mushrooms
1 cup cream
2 egg yolks
1 teaspoon lemon juice

Melt 2 tablespoons of the butter in a large saucepan. Put in the
pan the veal cubes, carrots, quartered onion, and salt. Cook,
uncovered, over very low heat, stirring occasionally, for 15
minutes (do not let the ingredients brown). Sprinkle 1 tablespoon of flour over all, blend well, and continue to cook over
low heat. After 5 minutes pour hot water (about 1 quart) into
the pan so that the ingredients are just covered. Add the bouquet garni and garlic. Cover, and simmer for 1½ hours or until
the veal is tender.

In another pan boil the small onions until just tender. Drain
and remove them. In the same pan sauté the mushrooms in 2
tablespoons of butter. When the veal is cooked, arrange the

cubes of meat, onions, and mushrooms on a hot platter, and keep warm in oven with door open.

Sauce (about 30 minutes to prepare): Strain the liquid in which the veal has cooked. Reduce 2 cups of this to 1 cup by boiling. Remove the pan from the heat and add the cream. Beat the egg yolks well in a bowl and then add a small amount of the warm broth to them. Add the lemon juice. Stir the egg mixture into the remaining broth and stir over very gentle heat until the sauce thickens (do not allow to boil). Add salt to taste and 1 tablespoon of butter. Pour the sauce over the veal, onions, and mushrooms. Serve with rice.

STUFFING FOR VEAL

(About 2 cups)

1 tablespoon butter
¼ cup minced onion
1 egg
½ lb. finely ground veal
½ lb. finely ground pork from Boston butt
¼ lb. finely ground fresh pork fat
½ teaspoon salt
¼ teaspoon pepper
¼ teaspoon dried thyme
½ or 1 clove garlic, mashed

Sauté the onions in the butter until transparent. Lightly beat the egg in a large bowl and to it add the ground veal, pork, and pork fat, salt, pepper, thyme, garlic and sautéed onions. Beat this mixture well with a wooden spoon until it is slightly fluffy. Stuff it into the roast and close the opening.

This is enough for a veal blade roast; for a veal breast, add about half again as much of each ingredient to the recipe. Double the recipe for a veal crown roast.

For lamb or pork crown roasts, double each ingredient, omit the veal entirely, and add 2 cups of soft bread crumbs that have been briefly soaked in 1 cup of beef bouillon and then drained. Add ¼ cup each of minced celery and parsley.

For lamb cushion shoulder and lamb rolled breast, change the ingredients as above for crown roasts, but prepare only half the amount of stuffing.

BROILED CALF'S LIVER WITH HERB BUTTER

(For 4)

1 lb. calf's liver, cut in slices ½ inch thick
4 to 5 tablespoons butter
1 tablespoon finely minced onion
1 teaspoon chopped parsley
½ teaspoon salt
⅛ teaspoon black pepper, freshly ground
2 teaspoons white-wine vinegar or lemon juice

Melt the butter in a small pan. Use about 1 tablespoon of it to coat the liver slices. Broil the slices 3 inches from moderate heat for about 2 to 3 minutes per side. In the remaining butter lightly sauté the onion and parsley. Add the salt, pepper, and vinegar or lemon juice. Blend well, and heat but do not allow to boil. Serve the liver slices on a hot platter, with the herb butter either poured over them or served separately.

SAUTÉED CALF'S LIVER WITH BASIL
(For 4)

1 lb. calf's liver, cut in slices ¼ to ⅓ inch thick
Salt and pepper
Flour
4 tablespoons butter
⅓ cup dry white wine
2 tablespoons beef consommé
1 teaspoon chopped parsley
¼ teaspoon dried basil

Season the liver slices with salt and pepper and dredge them with flour. Heat the butter in a skillet and sauté the liver in it over fairly high heat, allowing about 2 minutes per side. Remove the slices to a hot platter. Into the skillet pour the wine and the consomme, mix well, and bring to a light boil for about 1 minute. Add the parsley and basil and allow the sauce to boil gently for another minute. Pour the sauce over the liver slices.

VEAL KIDNEYS BORDEAUX
(For 4)

4 veal kidneys, cut into ½-inch slices
6 oz. salt pork, cut in ½-inch cubes
3 tablespoons butter
½ lb. fresh mushrooms, or 6-oz. can mushrooms, sliced
¼ cup dry red wine
1 cup Bordelaise Sauce made with red wine (see Index)
1 tablespoon chopped parsley

Parboil the salt pork cubes for 2 to 3 minutes and drain. Melt the butter in a large skillet and in it sauté together the salt pork and the mushrooms. When these are lightly browned, remove them to a warm platter. In the same butter sauté the kidney slices over lively heat, seasoning with pepper while they are cooking. When the kidneys have cooked approximately 5 to 6 minutes, remove them to the warm platter also. Pour the wine into the skillet and add the Bordelaise Sauce. Simmer 2 to 3 minutes, then add the mushrooms, salt pork and kidney slices. Blend well and heat thoroughly. Serve sprinkled with parsley.

VEAL KIDNEYS IN WHITE WINE

(For 4)

4 veal kidneys
Salt and pepper
4 tablespoons butter, in all
¼ cup dry white wine
1 teaspoon meat extract dissolved in ½ cup hot water
Lemon juice
1 tablespoon chopped parsley

Ask your meat cutter to leave a thin layer of suet around each kidney. Cut each one into 4 or 5 slices, wash in cold running water, and drain. Season the slices with salt and pepper and quickly sauté them over lively heat in 3 tablespoons of the butter. Remove the slices to a hot platter when they are done (5 or 6 minutes). Put the wine, dissolved meat extract, a generous squeeze of lemon juice, parsley, and 1 tablespoon of butter into the skillet. Heat, mixing well, and pour the sauce over the kidneys.

SWEETBREADS IN PARISIAN SAUCE

(For 4)

2 pairs sweetbreads
Several lardoons salt pork
2 tablespoons butter
1 medium onion, sliced
Pinch dried thyme
1/4 bay leaf
6 tablespoons veal or chicken stock
2 4-oz. cans mushrooms

Sauce:

Liquid from the mushrooms
2 egg yolks
5 tablespoons veal or chicken stock, cold
1 tablespoon flour kneaded with 1 tablespoon butter
Salt and pepper
Dash nutmeg
Lemon juice

Prepare sweetbreads for final cooking (see p. 177) and lard them with the salt pork.

In a casserole melt the butter and lay the slices of onion in it. Place the sweetbreads on top of the onion, add the thyme and bay leaf; cover the casserole. Cook over medium heat for about 5 minutes. Then add the veal or chicken stock, again cover the casserole, and place it in a 400° oven for 35 minutes. Baste the sweetbreads at least twice during the cooking, and when they are half done add the mushrooms.

Sauce: By boiling for about 5 minutes, reduce the liquid from the mushrooms by one half. Let cool. Beat the egg yolks lightly and mix them into the cooled mushroom liquid. Mix in the veal or chicken stock. When the sweetbreads are done, remove them and the mushrooms to a hot dish. Into the liquid remaining in the casserole stir the kneaded butter and flour and cook over low heat for 2 minutes. Turn off the heat under the casserole and slowly add the egg mixture, stirring constantly. Season with salt and pepper to taste, nutmeg, and a good squeeze of lemon juice. Then heat the sauce over low heat, stirring constantly, until it thickens. Do not allow to boil. When the sauce is thick, add the sweetbreads and mushrooms, and serve all from the casserole.

SWEETBREADS VILLEROI

(For 4)

- 2 pairs sweetbreads
- ½ cup Béchamel Sauce, cold (see Index)
- 2 egg yolks
- 1½ cups bread crumbs
- 2 eggs, beaten
- 2 tablespoons butter
- 2 tablespoons cooking oil

Prepare sweetbreads for final cooking (see p. 177). When they have been boiled and pressed, cut them crosswise into slices ⅓ inch thick.

Add the 2 egg yolks to the cold Béchamel Sauce and mix thoroughly. Dip the sweetbread slices first into the sauce, next into the bread crumbs, then into the beaten eggs, and, finally, again into the bread crumbs. Sauté the breaded slices in the combined butter and oil over lively heat, allowing about 5 minutes per side. Serve with green peas.

VEAL RING

(For 4 to 6)

1½ lbs. veal from the shoulder
1 medium onion
½ lb. pork from Boston butt
1 tablespoon parsley
1¼ teaspoons salt
¼ teaspoon pepper
Good dash nutmeg
⅓ cup Béchamel Sauce (see Index)
2 tablespoons heavy cream
2 eggs
1 egg yolk
1 cup Béarnaise Sauce (see Index)

Grind together at least twice the veal, onion, pork, and parsley. The mixture should be pasty. Mix in the salt, pepper, nutmeg, Béchamel Sauce, and cream. By hand, thoroughly blend in the 2 whole eggs and 1 egg yolk.

Press the mixture into a buttered 1½-quart or 6-cup ring mold (do not fill over two-thirds full). Place the mold in a pan of hot water, allowing the water to reach to the same height as the mixture inside the ring. Bake in a 325° oven for 1 hour. Let the ring cool for about 5 minutes before unmolding it.

Serve with the Béarnaise Sauce poured over the ring, and fill the center with potato balls that have been sautéed in butter.

Note: The ring mixture may be prepared several hours before cooking. Store, tightly covered, in the refrigerator, and let stand at room temperature about ½ hour before placing in the oven.

CHAPTER 12

LAMB

Since about 90 per cent of all the fresh meat from sheep consumed in the United States is meat from lambs, this chapter will deal almost entirely with lamb meat.

A lamb is a young sheep of either sex that has not reached maturity. Lambs for the meat market are divided into four groups:

1) Hothouse lamb—a lamb that has been raised very carefully, housed in a barn, and consequently sheltered from the cold. They are slaughtered between the ages of six to ten weeks and usually weigh between 30 and 40 pounds hog-dressed (all viscera but the kidneys are removed, the carcass is whole, and the head and pelt remain on the carcass). The supply of hothouse lambs is small and meat from them is quite expensive.

2) Genuine spring lamb—milk-fed lamb marketed in the spring and early summer. The age qualification for this group is three to five months. There is only one breed of sheep, the Dorset, to which lambs can be born at almost any time of the year; thus, there can be only a small supply of genuine spring lamb in seasons of the year other than spring and early summer.

LAMB BONE CHART

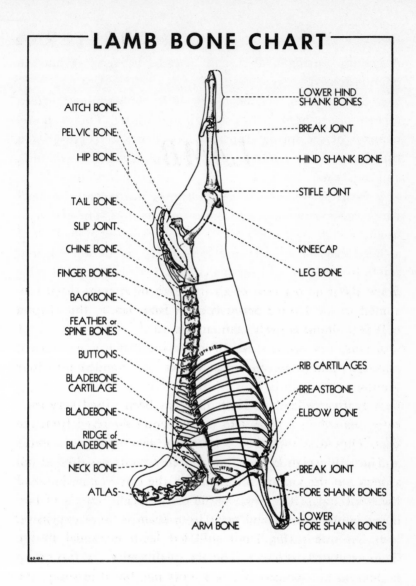

AITCH BONE

PELVIC BONE

HIP BONE

TAIL BONE

SLIP JOINT

CHINE BONE

FINGER BONES

BACKBONE

FEATHER or
SPINE BONES

BUTTONS

BLADEBONE
CARTILAGE

BLADEBONE

RIDGE of
BLADEBONE

NECK BONE

ATLAS

ARM BONE

13TH RIB

1ST RIB

LOWER HIND
SHANK BONES

BREAK JOINT

HIND SHANK BONE

STIFLE JOINT

KNEECAP

LEG BONE

RIB CARTILAGES

BREASTBONE

ELBOW BONE

BREAK JOINT

FORE SHANK BONES

LOWER
FORE SHANK BONES

NATIONAL LIVE STOCK AND MEAT BOARD

A genuine spring lamb usually weighs between 35 and 50 pounds dressed.

3) Spring lamb, or just plain lamb—lamb under fourteen months of age marketed in the fall and winter. This is the remainder of the spring crop that has been allowed to grow a little older. These lambs have subsisted on feed other than milk and they usually weigh between 70 and 90 pounds dressed.

4) Yearling lamb or yearling mutton—a nearly mature animal whose age is between fifteen and twenty months. These animals usually weigh 90 to 100 pounds and over dressed. The meat of a sheep that is over twenty months of age is mutton. Mutton comes from either wethers (males castrated when young lambs) or ewes (females that have borne at least one lamb).

Sheep are raised for two purposes—meat and wool—and some breeds have proved to be better than others for either food or wool purposes. Medium-wool sheep such as Southdown (named after the downs, or treeless chalky hills, of the southern coast of England), Shropshire, Hampshire, and Oxford, are among the best meat producers.

❀ Lamb of Good Quality: What to Look for

The color of the lean meat varies with the age of the animal, becoming darker with increasing age. Young, milk-fed lamb will have light pink lean; genuine spring lamb will have deeper pink lean; average market lamb will have pinkish-red lean; and yearling lamb will have light-red to medium-red lean. The texture of the lean should always be fine and velvety. The fat should be smooth, firm, white, somewhat brittle but of a waxy consistency. The exterior fat is covered with a parchment-like tissue called the fell, which helps keep the wholesale cut fresh and protects it if the lamb is aged. By the time the lamb reaches the meat counter the fell usually has been removed from all cuts but the leg. Most cookbooks fall into one of three classes: those that tell you definitely to remove the fell, those that tell you definitely to leave it on, and those that ignore the whole issue. Actually, it makes no difference what you do as far as flavor is concerned; the fell does not affect it. But marinade and other seasonings will penetrate more easily the roast from which the fell has been removed.

Lamb bones are porous and red. If you have a chance to inspect the forelegs of a lamb, you will see what is called the break joint—the point at which the feet are removed. This joint is slightly above the real foot joint. In young lambs the break joint will have four red, moist, and porous ridges. In older lambs these ridges become hard and white. When a sheep reaches the mutton stage, the foot cannot be removed at the break joint and instead is removed at the real joint, called the spool joint because of its appearance. Hind legs also have break joints, but these are more difficult to see in the retail cut.

✾ How Lamb Is Cut

The carcass is seldom split into sides as is beef, although for clarity and easier comparison the Lamb Cut Chart on p. 198 pictures it this way. More often it is divided in half crosswise, producing a hindsaddle and a foresaddle, as in veal; or a very young lamb remains whole, as does a hog-dressed hothouse lamb. Still another way of dividing a lamb is into legs, loin, hotel rack (rib section), and stew (breast and flank).

LAMB CUT CHART

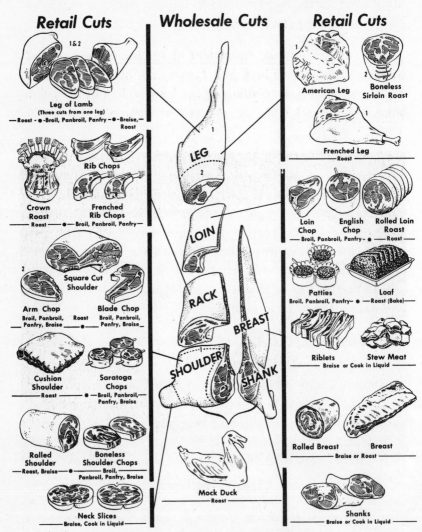

Retail Cuts

1 & 2

Leg of Lamb
(Three cuts from one leg)
— Roast - ● -Broil, Panbroil, Panfry - ● -Braise,—
Roast

Rib Chops

Crown Roast
— Roast —

Frenched Rib Chops
— ● — Broil, Panbroil, Panfry —

2

Square Cut Shoulder

Arm Chop
Broil, Panbroil, Panfry, Braise

Roast
●

Blade Chop
Broil, Panbroil, Panfry, Braise

Cushion Shoulder
— Roast —

Saratoga Chops
● —Broil, Panbroil,—
Panfry, Braise

Rolled Shoulder
— Roast, Braise — ●

Boneless Shoulder Chops
— Broil,
Panbroil, Panfry, Braise

Neck Slices
— Braise, Cook in Liquid —

Wholesale Cuts

LEG
1
2

LOIN

RACK

BREAST

SHOULDER

SHANK

Mock Duck
— Roast —

Retail Cuts

1

American Leg

2

Boneless Sirloin Roast

1

Frenched Leg
— Roast —

Loin Chop   **English Chop**   **Rolled Loin Roast**
— Broil, Panbroil, Panfry — ●   — Roast —

Patties
Broil, Panbroil, Panfry — ●

Loaf
— Roast (Bake) —

Riblets   **Stew Meat**
— Braise or Cook in Liquid —

Rolled Breast   **Breast**
— Braise or Roast —

Shanks
— Braise or Cook in Liquid —

NATIONAL LIVE STOCK AND MEAT BOARD

Hindsaddle

LEG—Wholesale Cut

This cut contains the equivalent of the hind shank, round, rump, and sirloin of beef (see Lamb and Beef Cut Charts). Sometimes the sirloin, containing the forward half of the pelvic bone and the tail bone, is removed to make a separate cut.

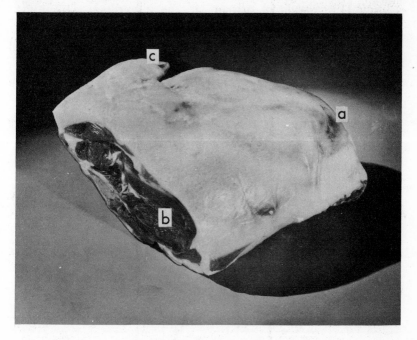

AMERICAN LEG

The meat is peeled back from the shank bone at the stifle joint and the bone is removed (a). The meat is then folded into place, covered with the fell, and fastened (see Lamb Cut Chart).

(b) The face of the cut will somewhat resemble a beef sirloin steak, since this leg has been cut upward through the sirloin. (c) The tail of the animal.

It is also possible to buy only half a leg, either the shank half or the loin half—the shank half being the less tender of the two, but the loin half being a little more difficult to carve.

To roast: The leg should be roasted, since lamb is a tender meat. For a nice flavor, either marinate the leg (see Chapter 7), adding ¼ teaspoon of orégano to the ingredients. Or, insert slivers of garlic into small incisions made with a pointed knife. Season with salt and pepper before roasting if you wish. Roast in a 300° or 325° oven, counting on 20 to 35 minutes per pound, depending on the size of the cut and the thermometer reading you want to reach. The thermometer should read 175° for a medium well-done leg and 180° for a well-done leg. If you have extremely high-quality lamb and if you like your meat nicely pink and juicy, remove the leg from the oven when the thermometer reads 160° to 165°.

Pardon me, but my personal taste is showing: Serve mint sauce or mint jelly with leg of lamb if you must, but I much prefer serving it with its own juices (reduced if there is enough of them) and slices of lemon, especially if the leg has had garlic added to it. Lamb is delicious by itself and mint has a pretty powerful flavor!

Frenched Leg. In meat circles, "to French" means to bare a bone, usually for an inch or so, to provide space for little paper pantaloons, or frills, that are put on after cooking. These pantaloons do have a purpose other than decoration. The custom of using them harks back to the Middle Ages when women, who generally did not eat with the men at banquets and such, had the carving responsibilities bestowed upon them. The paper pantaloons enabled them to grasp the bone for easier carving without dirtying their fingers. Today's men do not like greasy fingers either, although now a fork is generally used to keep the roast in check.

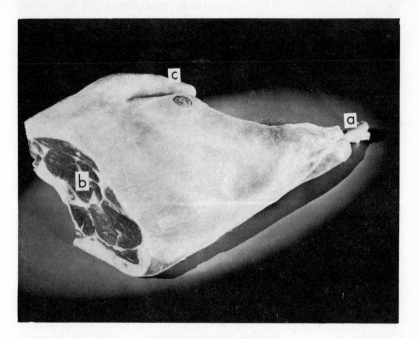

FRENCHED LEG

A lamb leg is Frenched by removing the meat on the shank (a). See the Lamb Cut Chart for a better picture. (b) The face resembles a beef sirloin steak. (c) The tail of the animal.

Roast as you would any leg of lamb, but wrap a slice of bacon or a piece of aluminum foil around the exposed bone to protect it.

Paper Frills: You can make your own pantaloon by folding a piece of white paper measuring 11 inches by approximately 4 inches. Work from one of the 4-inch ends: Fold it up from the bottom 1½ inches, crease it, and 1¼ inches above the crease fold the long end of the paper back and down. Two inches from the second crease fold the long end back and up; 1¼ inches from that, fold it back and down again. Finally, 2 inches from the last crease, fold the paper back and up. You should then have three "pleats" in front and plain paper in back. Trim the two 4-inch ends so they are even with the first inside crease. Now cut a series of slits along each pleat, making them neatly at right angles to the edge of the pleat, about ½ inch deep, and very close together. "Blouse" them after they are cut by lightly pressing down on them with your hand. Wrap the frill around the bone to try it for size and cut off any extra. Slip one end inside the last fold at the other end, and fasten at the bottom with Scotch Tape. Now, when your leg of lamb is done, just slip the pantaloon over the bone and there you are.

Leg Chops or Steaks. The description of these slices depends on where in the leg they are cut. Some will resemble beef round steaks (p. 98) having a small round bone as their distinctive feature. Others will contain cross sections of the aitchbone and backbone. It is sometimes difficult to buy these steaks, since a meat market may not want to cut into a leg of lamb to make them.

Leg steaks may be broiled, panbroiled, or sautéed; see under loin chops further on for cooking instructions.

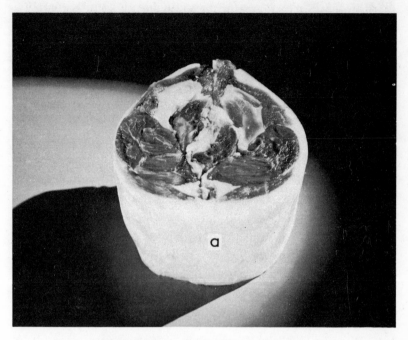

BONELESS SIRLOIN ROAST

The sirloin section is divided from the legs, and it is boned and rolled. It is a cross section of the carcass—both sides of the animal are in the cut. The roast will weigh around 2 to 3½ pounds after it has been rolled. (a) The backbone will have been removed from along here.

Roast as you would a leg, allowing about 10 minutes more time per pound because the cut is rolled.

Sirloin Chops. (See photograph on next page.) These chops look like miniature beef sirloin steaks, and they, too, will vary in shape and amount of bone according to where they are cut

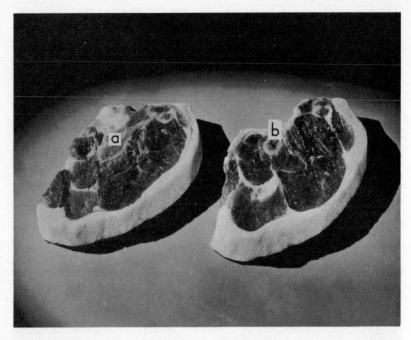

SIRLOIN CHOPS

in the sirloin section. (a) The larger part of the pelvic bone. (b) The smaller round part of the pelvic bone.

Cook these chops as you would cook any lamb chop. See under loin chops further on.

LOIN—*Wholesale Cut*

This cut corresponds to the short loin of beef (see Lamb and Beef Cut Charts). It also contains the thirteenth rib. The loin may be left whole when it is put in the meat-market display case, enabling you to get two identical chops from every slice you order. It may also be split along the backbone, yielding single chops with T-shaped bones. The loin is the choice section of lamb as far as chops are concerned. There is little bone and comparatively much lean.

LOIN ROAST

One side of the entire loin section is pictured in the photograph. You also can buy the whole section—a cross section of the carcass—for a roast twice this size. (a) The beginning of the loin "eye" muscle, and (b) the tenderloin muscle. (The face of the roast here shows the side nearest the sirloin section.) (c) The lean of the end of the breast (corresponds to the flank of beef). (d) The fat that will eventually surround the kidneys.

Roast the loin as you would a leg.

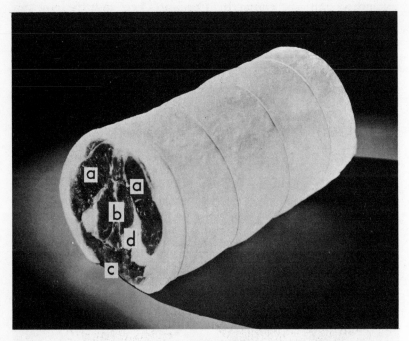

ROLLED LOIN

The cut in the photograph is a cross section from the carcass of the entire loin which has been boned and rolled. (a) Both loin "eye" muscles. (b) Both tenderloin muscles. (c) Both "tails." (d) The channel or kidney fat. Roast the rolled loin as you would a leg, allowing about 10 minutes more per pound because it is rolled.

Loin Chops. These are slices from 1 to 2 inches thick cut from the loin. They will resemble a beef porterhouse, T-bone, or club steak depending on from what portion of the section they come. The chops in the photograph look like miniature porterhouse steaks (p. 109). (a) The backbone with the finger bone extending into the chop. (b) The loin "eye" muscle. (c) The tenderloin muscle. (d) The channel fat. (e) The "tail." Loin chops are usually higher in price than rib chops because of the

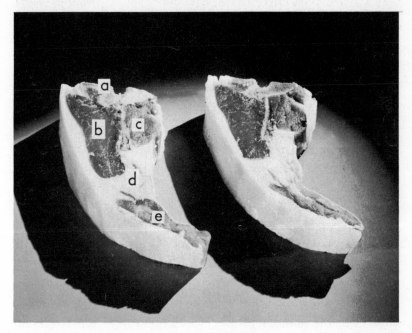

LOIN CHOPS

smaller amount of bone and the greater amount of tender lean they contain.

To cook: The best way, I think, to cook a loin or rib chop is to broil it, although you can also panbroil or sauté it. Lamb chops should not be cooked to death—they should be juicy and slightly pink in the center.

There are two methods of broiling chops: 1) Sear them

quickly on both sides under high (500°) heat, then reduce the
heat to 350° and cook until done; 2) broil them under a constant 350° heat. In both methods the chops should be 2 to 3
inches from the heat, the thicker ones requiring the 3 inches.

| *At 350°* | | | *Searing Method* | |
Thickness	Min. per Side		Thickness	Min. per Side after Searing
1 inch	6		1 inch	4-5
1½ inches	9		1½ inches	6-7
2 inches	11		2 inches	8-10

It is difficult to give times on panbroiling, but usually the
cooking time will be less than for real broiling. Be sure to pour
off excess fat as it accumulates. A little fat or butter rubbed on
the skillet before cooking the chops will prevent initial sticking.

For the most part, serving a sauce with lamb chops will only
detract from their flavor. Salt and pepper and a sprig of parsley
for color are all that is necessary. Sautéed, broiled, or stuffed
tomatoes, and mushrooms that have been sautéed in butter,
make a nice accompaniment. And, of course, any green vegetable goes well with chops.

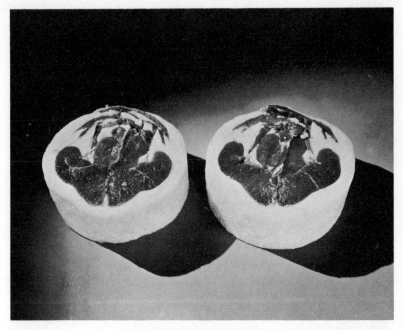

ENGLISH CHOPS

These chops are cross-sectional slices from the whole loin. The backbone is removed and the chop is held together with a skewer. Actually, these chops are simply slices of a rolled loin (see rolled loin above for identification of muscles, etc.). The English chop often contains the kidney, which is usually fastened into the middle of the chop, and the slice is generally a rather thick one. Cut from the finest mutton, these chops are considered a special delicacy by serious amateurs of meat.

FORESADDLE

RACK—Wholesale Cut

This section is sometimes called the hotel rack. It contains eight or nine pairs of ribs. It is usually split in half down the backbone.

RIB ROAST

The rack is comparable to the beef standing rib (p. 117). (a) The rib "eye" muscle. Roast this cut as you would the leg; cooking time may be 5 to 10 minutes less per pound. The final thermometer reading should be 175° to 180° for medium-well or well done; less, to your taste, for pink.

Crown Roast. (See photograph on following page.) This is the fancy way of serving the rack. It is an impressive sight, especially when each rib end, which has been Frenched, is covered with a paper pantaloon (see p. 202), and the hole in the center is brimming with such things as French-fried potato balls, green peas, or a bouquet of water cress. Twelve to sixteen ribs make a crown.

Your meat cutter will prepare the roast for you. Prepare for cooking by covering the rib ends with cubes of salt pork, raw potato, or a wrapping of aluminum foil. You may fill the center with a flavorful stuffing (see Index) or leave it empty to be filled, after cooking, with a vegetable. If you do leave it empty, it is a good idea to put a Pyrex or metal bowl or pan in the space to help the roast hold its shape.

Be sure to use a meat thermometer, for the cooking time might be less than for other roasts. The thermometer should still read 175° to 180°, or 170° or less if you belong to the pink school.

Rib Chops. (See photograph on following page.) These chops are cut to contain at least one rib. Usually, a one-rib chop will be about an inch thick. (a) The backbone. (b) The rib. (c) The rib "eye" muscle. There is more bone, about the same amount of fat, and slightly less lean in a rib chop than in a loin chop.

Broil or panbroil a rib chop as you would a loin chop. You may sauté it too.

Rib chops can be Frenched. If they are, protect the bone while broiling by wrapping a bit of bacon or aluminum foil

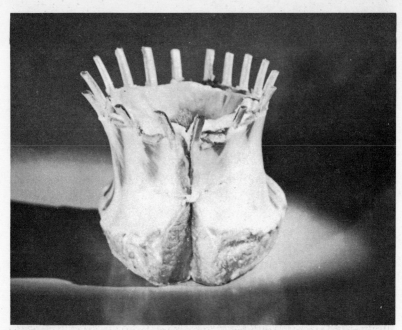

CROWN ROAST

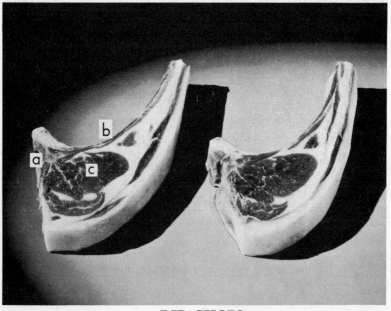

RIB CHOPS

around it. Paper frills here serve no practical purpose (unless you intend to eat the chop with your fingers!) and are just for show.

Rib chops can also be made to look like Saratoga chops (see under shoulder, below). The rib and backbone are removed and the tail is rolled around the rib "eye." A skewer holds everything in place. The layers of lean and fat encircling the "eye" make these chops an attractive variation.

SHOULDER—*Wholesale Cut*

This is the same cut as a beef chuck (see Lamb and Beef Cut Charts) except that the lamb shoulder usually contains only

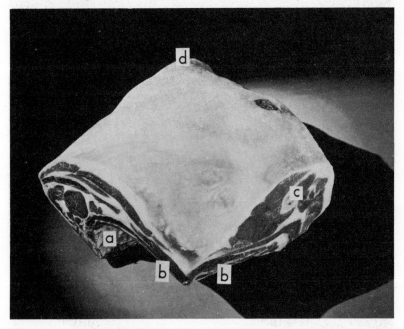

SQUARE-CUT SHOULDER

three or four ribs—or pairs of ribs if the shoulder is a cross section cut from the whole carcass. As in the beef chuck, the several muscles in this section run in many directions.

Square-Cut Shoulder. (See photograph on preceding page.) There shouldn't be much confusion about the identification of this cut. (a) The backbone. (b) The rib and cross-cut sections of it. (c) The arm bone. (d) The neck is removed here. You may roast the shoulder as is, but, as you can well imagine, it could be a carver's nightmare! The cooking time will be 30 to 35 minutes per pound and the meat thermometer should read 175° to 180°.

Cushion Shoulder. A much smarter buy. All the bones have been removed. In the photograph you can see that the shoulder has been sewn together on the two open sides. You may ask your meat cutter to leave one side open so that you can add a stuffing (see Index). It will take 2 to 3 cups of stuffing, depending on the size of the shoulder. Sew or skewer the opening after the shoulder has been stuffed.

Roasting may take a bit longer than an ordinary roast. Count on about 35 to 40 minutes per pound. Thermometer reading should be 175° to 180°.

Rolled Shoulder. The shoulder boned again, but here formed into a compact roll. Roast the rolled shoulder to a thermometer reading of 175° to 180°. Cooking time should be 40 to 45 minutes per pound. Remember that slips of garlic inserted at intervals into the lean add a nice flavor. Or marinate the roast before cooking (see Chapter 7).

CUSHION SHOULDER

ROLLED SHOULDER

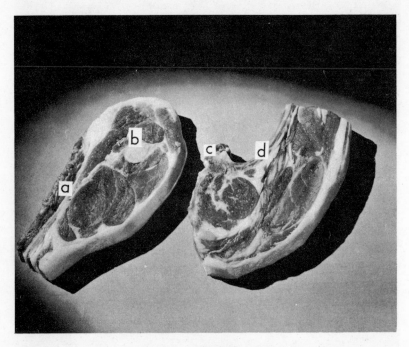

SHOULDER CHOPS

The chop on the left is cut from the arm. (a) Cross sections of
the first ribs. (b) Cross section of the arm bone. On the right is
a blade chop. (c) The backbone. (d) A rib. Blade chops may
also include a cross section of the bladebone. Both these chops
have more muscles than loin or rib chops and consequently
more thick connective tissue. The blade chop may contain a
good deal of bone. The fat content of these chops is comparatively less than in loin or rib chops.

You may broil or panbroil arm or blade shoulder chops as
you would a loin or rib chop, but you may find that sautéing

them in a small amount of butter is more satisfactory. If you sauté, season the chop with salt and pepper on both sides before cooking. Sautéed shoulder chops are good served with Curry Sauce (see Index).

SARATOGA CHOPS

The shoulder chop here has been boned and rolled. The chop is composed generally of the inside shoulder muscle. Cook as you would an ordinary shoulder chop.

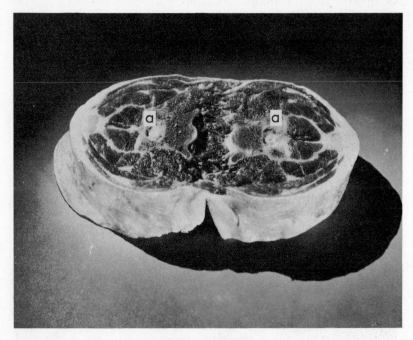

NECK SLICES

The lamb neck contains a fair amount of lean meat. The cut
in the photograph is a cross-sectional slice that has been almost
split in half and then the two halves laid flat. (a) The neck bone.
Because the neck muscles are much used, they are not as
tender as most lamb muscles. Neck slices should be braised.
Brown the slices quickly in butter, reduce the heat, add a little
water or white wine, and cook, covered, for about an hour.

BREAST—Wholesale Cut

This cut corresponds to the short plate, brisket, and shank
of beef (see Lamb and Beef Cut Charts). It contains the ends

of twelve ribs, the breastbone, and the shank bones. There is as much fat in the breast as there is lean and about 10 per cent of the cut is bone.

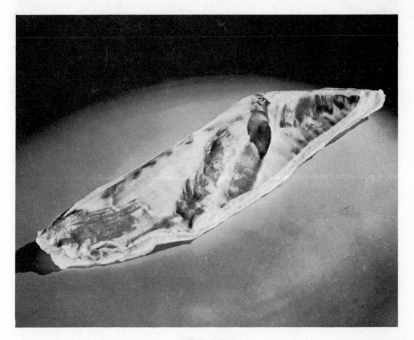

BREAST

A rather cumbersome cut, to say the least. Have your meat cutter cut the breast into serving pieces or riblets (see veal riblets, p. 173) so that you can braise (see below) or simmer it more easily. Braising and simmering times will be about 1½ to 2 hours.

ROLLED BREAST

This cut resembles a jelly roll because of the layers of lean and
fat. Ask your meat cutter to leave it untied if you plan to roll
a stuffing in it. Or buy it unrolled and simply season the flat
piece with salt, pepper, chopped parsley, and a sliced clove of
garlic. If you plan to stuff the breast, you may use either a bread
stuffing or a ground-pork stuffing (see Index). The stuffing
should be spread over the flat meat, then the meat should be
tightly rolled and securely fastened at intervals with string.

A rolled breast can be roasted or braised. Roasting time will
be about 35 minutes per pound and the thermometer reading
should be 175° to 180°. Braising time will be 1½ to 2 hours.

When braising, try white wine diluted with a bit of water as the liquid, and add to the pot one half a bay leaf, a pinch of dried thyme, a clove of garlic, and a branch of parsley (remove these herbs when and if you thicken the liquid for gravy). Vegetables such as carrots and tiny onions are also a nice addition to the braising pot.

SHANK

The shank contains the elbow bone and the foreshank bones. Count on one shank per person. Braise shanks, remembering that bay leaf, thyme, parsley, and garlic added to the liquid as before contribute to the flavor. Cooking time will be about 1½ hours.

VARIETY MEATS

The liver, heart, tongue, brains, and sweetbreads of lamb can be prepared and cooked as you would prepare and cook these organs for veal (see pp. 174-177 and Index).

Kidney. The lamb kidney looks exactly like a glorified kidney bean. It lacks the lobulations of beef or veal kidneys. You should count on three lamb kidneys per person.

Lamb kidneys can be cooked in the same manner as veal kidneys, but instead of slicing lamb kidneys, you need only cut them in half lengthwise, remove the white cores with scissors, then wash them.

A nice way to broil kidneys is to split them not quite enough to sever the halves. Keep the halves open by threading them side by side on a small metal skewer. Dip each kidney in butter and sprinkle it with salt. Broil quickly under a high heat for about 3 minutes on each side. When done, remove the skewer and fill the kidney's center with a ball of softened butter into which you have mixed chopped parsley, a squeeze of lemon juice, salt and pepper, and a pinch of dry mustard.

All the sauces for veal kidney can (and should) be used for lamb kidney—Bordelaise, Hunter's, Mushroom, etc. (see Index).

GROUND LAMB

Usually ground lamb comes from the flank, breast, shank, and neck. It can be made into patties or combined with other ground meat to make a meat loaf (see recipes at the end of this chapter).

Lamb Recipes

LAMB ROLLS IN WHITE WINE

(For 4)

1 to 1½ lbs. lamb steak, sliced or pounded ¼ inch thick
4 tablespoons butter, in all
1 onion, sliced thin
1 to 2 cloves garlic, slivered
Flour
Salt and pepper
Pinch rosemary
½ cup dry white wine

Cut the thin steaks into 3-inch squares. Lightly sauté the onion slices in 1 tablespoon of butter. Sprinkle one side of each lamb square with salt and pepper, and on each place a sautéed onion slice and a sliver of garlic. Roll the squares and fasten them with toothpicks or string. Dredge with flour seasoned with a little salt and pepper.

Melt the remaining butter in a skillet, and sauté the rolls in it over medium heat until they are golden brown. Sprinkle the rosemary over the rolls and continue cooking, uncovered, in a 325° oven for 15 minutes, or until the meat is tender. Remove the rolls to a hot platter, and stir the wine into the skillet. Bring the wine to a boil, simmer for a minute or so, and then pour over the lamb rolls.

BROILED MARINATED LAMB CHOPS
(For 4)

4 thick lamb chops, preferably from loin or rib
¼ cup olive oil
½ teaspoon dry mustard
1 tablespoon white-wine vinegar
1 clove garlic, sliced
3 peppercorns, crushed

Mix the mustard with the olive oil; add the vinegar, garlic, and peppercorns. Arrange the lamb chops on a plate so that they do not overlap. Pour the marinade over them and leave the chops to marinate for at least an hour, turning them often enough to keep them moist. To broil the chops, see time table earlier in this chapter or in the Appendix.

LAMB CHOPS WITH ONION PURÉE
(For 4)

4 rib lamb chops, cut thick
4 to 6 slices bacon
2 tablespoons butter

Onion purée:

2 onions, minced
2 tablespoons butter
¼ teaspoon salt
2 tablespoons rice
¼ cup boiling beef bouillon
2 tablespoons thick Béchamel Sauce (see Index)

Onion purée: Melt the butter in a saucepan. Add the minced onions and cover the pan. Cook over low heat for about 5 minutes. Add salt, rice, and bouillon; mix, re-cover the pan, and continue cooking for about 15 minutes or until the rice absorbs the liquid. When all the liquid has disappeared, force the mixture through a sieve. Bind it together with the thick Béchamel Sauce.

Remove the rib and excess fat from each chop. Encircle the edges of the chop with a bacon strip and fasten in place with a toothpick. Melt the butter in a skillet and sauté each chop on one side only; cook to a golden brown. Now turn the chops and spread the browned side of each one with onion purée. Finish the cooking, uncovered, in a 325° oven. This should take 15 to 20 minutes, depending on the thickness of the chop.

LAMB CHOPS IN A CRUST

(For 4)

4 lamb chops, loin or rib, cut fairly thick
Salt and pepper
6-oz. can mushrooms
1 clove garlic
1 egg, lightly beaten

Crust:
1¼ cups sifted flour
Salt and pepper
6 tablespoons butter
1 egg yolk
Ice water, about 5 tablespoons

Remove the bone from the chops, or have the meat cutter remove them. Salt and pepper each chop and panbroil them for 2 minutes on each side. Remove from the pan and allow them to cool. Mince the mushrooms and garlic together until quite fine.

Crust: Add a tiny pinch each of salt and pepper to the flour in a bowl. Cut in the butter as you would for a pie crust. When the flour and butter have reached the small-pellet stage, quickly blend in the egg yolk with your finger tips. Stir in the ice water bit by bit. The dough should be quite firm. Roll it out to pie-crust thickness, and cut it into squares, each large enough to completely surround a chop, with enough extra to seal the crust around the edge.

Spread each chop on both sides with a thin coating of the mushroom-garlic mince, and then enclose the chop in a pastry square, sealing the edges together by moistening with water and folding or pressing with fingers. Brush the tops of the crusts with the lightly beaten egg. Bake in a 375° oven for 30 minutes.

BOINJTEE BRIEDI

(For 4)

This is a South African stew, pronounced "boin-kee bree-dee." The Afrikaans name translated into English is "bean stew." A very good friend, Charlotte Murray, who has been living in Transvaal for the past few years, cooked this stew for me on her recent visit to America.

    1 lb. shoulder lamb chops
    Salt and pepper
    1 tablespoon butter
    ½ medium onion, minced

    2 medium potatoes, sliced thin
    2 large tomatoes, peeled and chopped
    ½ lb. green beans, cooked
    2 to 3 tablespoons sugar

Salt and pepper the chops. In a skillet, brown them over medium heat in the butter. When brown, sprinkle the onion over them, cover the skillet, and simmer for 30 minutes. Then add the potato slices and tomatoes, and simmer for another 30 minutes. Add the beans and sugar, and simmer for a final 30 minutes.

Wheat groats are traditionally served with this stew in South Africa, but rice is a good substitute.

LAMB SHOULDER MARIETTE

(For 4 or 6)

    1 lamb cushion shoulder *

    Stuffing:

    1 lb. sausage meat
    1 onion, minced
    1 clove garlic, minced
    1 tablespoon chopped parsley
    1 egg, lightly beaten
    1 cup bread crumbs
    1 teaspoon salt
    ½ teaspoon pepper

    2 tablespoons fat from cooked sausage
    1 onion, quartered
    1 carrot, cut in 4 pieces

  * If the shoulder is small, use only one half of all ingredients.

1 clove garlic
½ cup water
2 tablespoons flour

Stuffing: Lightly sauté the sausage meat. Remove from the heat, and drain off and reserve all but ⅓ cup of the fat. Make a stuffing by adding to the sausage the minced onion, garlic, and parsley, the egg, bread crumbs, salt, and pepper. Stuff this into the shoulder and sew up the open edges (see photograph, p. 215).

In a deep kettle brown the shoulder in the 2 tablespoons of the reserved fat. Add the onion and carrot. When these are nicely colored, add the garlic clove and water. Cover the kettle and simmer for 2 to 2½ hours, or until the meat is tender.

When the shoulder is done, place it on a hot platter. Remove the vegetables from the liquid in the kettle and skim off the fat. In a saucepan blend together a generous spoonful of the fat, and the flour, then stir in the cooking juices. Let this gravy simmer for 2 or 3 minutes, stirring often, and serve in a sauceboat.

CURRIED LAMB SHANKS

(For 4)

4 lamb shanks
3 to 4 tablespoons flour
2 teaspoons paprika
Salt and pepper
5 tablespoons butter, in all
1 clove garlic, sliced
1 bay leaf, crushed
Pinch dried thyme
1 cup water
1 tablespoon curry powder

Combine the flour, paprika, and a good sprinkling of salt and pepper. Dredge the shanks with this. Melt 3 tablespoons of the butter in a large heavy skillet, and in it lightly sauté the garlic. Brown the shanks on all sides in the same butter, and then sprinkle the crushed bay leaf and thyme over them. Pour the water into the skillet, cover, and simmer for 1 to 1½ hours, or until the meat is tender. Remove the shanks to a hot platter, and strain the remaining liquid through a sieve. Melt the remaining 2 tablespoons of butter in a saucepan, and stir in the remaining seasoned flour. Slowly add the liquid and cook, stirring often, until the sauce thickens. Add the curry, blend well, and add more salt if necessary. Pour the sauce over the shanks and serve with rice.

AVIGNON LAMB STEW

(For 4)

2 lbs. lamb shoulder, cut into 2-inch cubes
Lardoons of salt pork (as many lardoons as cubes)
Marinade (see Index), made with 1 cup red wine
4 ozs. salt pork, cut into small cubes
2 tomatoes, peeled, seeded, and chopped

Lard each lamb cube with a lardoon of salt pork (see Chapter 7), and marinate the cubes overnight.

In a large casserole place the lamb cubes and on top of them the small cubes of salt pork and the tomatoes. Pour the marinade, including all its vegetables, over all. Cover the casserole tightly and cook in a 325° oven for 2 to 3 hours. Halfway through the cooking period taste to see if salt should be added. If, when the stew is done, there seems to be excess fat on top, skim it off before serving. Serve in the casserole.

LAMB KIDNEYS BORDELAISE

(For 4)

12 lamb kidneys, split in half lengthwise
12 thin strips of salt pork, about 2 inches long
3/4 cup Bordelaise Sauce (see Index)
4 to 5 large fresh mushrooms, or 4-oz. can mushrooms
4 tablespoons butter
Salt and pepper

Put the strips of salt pork in a skillet or saucepan with 2 table-spoons of hot water. Cover the pan, bring the water to a boil, and cook the salt pork for 2 minutes. Pour off any excess water, then brown the salt pork, uncovered, in the skillet. Add the Bordelaise Sauce and the mushrooms, which have first been lightly sautéed in 1 tablespoon of the butter. Simmer together for 20 minutes. Wash and drain the kidney halves and sprinkle them lightly with salt and pepper. In the remaining 3 table-spoons of butter sauté them for 2 to 3 minutes per side. Place them on a hot platter and pour the sauce over them.

LAMB KIDNEYS CHASSEUR

(For 4)

12 lamb kidneys
Salt and pepper
Flour
4 tablespoons butter
1 cup Hunter's Sauce (see Index), made with 3/4 lb. mush-rooms instead of 1/2 lb.

Cut the kidneys crosswise into slices 1/3 inch thick. Wash in cold water and drain. Season the slices with salt and pepper and dredge them with flour. Sauté quickly, about 2 minutes per side, in the butter. Remove the kidney slices to a hot platter. Heat the Hunter's Sauce in the skillet, and serve it either separately or poured over the meat.

RUSSIAN LAMB PATTIES

(For 4)

1½ lbs. ground lamb
5 tablespoons butter, in all
½ teaspoon salt, slightly heaping
Pepper
Flour
2 eggs, lightly beaten
¾ to 1 cup bread crumbs
1 medium onion, minced
½ cup sour cream

Combine the lamb, 1 tablespoon of the butter, salt, and a sprinkle of pepper. Form into patties. Dredge each patty with flour, dip it in the beaten eggs, and then in the bread crumbs. Sauté the patties in 3 tablespoons of the butter over medium heat for about 20 minutes. When they are done, sprinkle with the minced onion that has been browned in the remaining tablespoon of butter. Remove the patties to a hot platter. Heat the sour cream in the skillet in which the meat has cooked, but do not let it boil. Pour the sour cream over the patties and serve.

LAMB LOAF

(For 4)

1 onion, minced
½ green pepper, minced
1 clove garlic, minced
2 tablespoons chopped parsley
2 tablespoons butter
1½ lbs. ground lamb
¼ lb. ground pork (preferably from Boston butt)
1 cup bread crumbs
1 teaspoon salt, heaping
Pepper
2 eggs

Sauté the onion, green pepper, garlic, and parsley in the butter for 3 to 4 minutes. With your hands combine this mixture with all the remaining ingredients. Bake, well-packed in a buttered loaf pan, in a 350° oven for 1¼ hours.

CHAPTER 13

PORK

Pork comes from two types of hogs, butcher and bacon. Americans eat the pork of butcher-type hogs—animals with rather short legs and thick, rounded torsos. The English, on the other hand, like their pork from bacon-type hogs—animals with longer legs and a lanky, narrow body; these hogs yield a pork with much less fat. There is an increasing trend in this country, however, to produce leaner butcher-type hogs.

Most of the pork you eat comes from animals between five to seven months of age that weigh around 200 to 225 pounds when they come to market. Since the hogs are under a year of age when slaughtered, it makes no difference whether the meat comes from barrows (males castrated when young) or gilts (young females).

Pork ranks next to beef (which comes first) in the amount consumed in the United States; some sections of the country—Chicago and the Minneapolis-St. Paul area, for instance—consume much more pork than other sections do. The amount of cured pork versus fresh pork consumed varies also. The northern half of the United States eats far more fresh pork and the southern half far more cured pork.

PORK BONE CHART

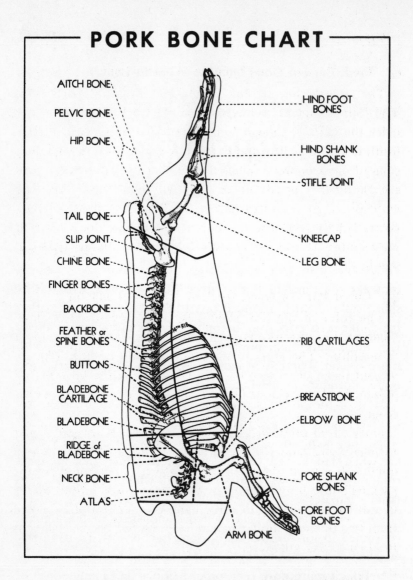

AITCH BONE

PELVIC BONE

HIP BONE

TAIL BONE

SLIP JOINT

CHINE BONE

FINGER BONES

BACKBONE

FEATHER or SPINE BONES

BUTTONS

BLADEBONE CARTILAGE

BLADEBONE

RIDGE of BLADEBONE

NECK BONE

ATLAS

HIND FOOT BONES

HIND SHANK BONES

STIFLE JOINT

KNEECAP

LEG BONE

RIB CARTILAGES

BREASTBONE

ELBOW BONE

FORE SHANK BONES

FORE FOOT BONES

ARM BONE

NATIONAL LIVE STOCK AND MEAT BOARD

❀ Fresh Pork of Good Quality: What to Look for

The fat covering of pork should be white and fairly firm. The lean should be a grayish-pink (the darker the color, the older the animal, though some breeds naturally yield a dark lean); it should be firm and have a fine grain. Even though pork comes from a young animal, the muscles of high-quality pork are marbled. The advantage of fat in pork cannot be over-emphasized. As I said earlier in the book, the flavor of pork comes largely from the fat. For heaven's sake, don't let your meat cutter trim off every little bit of fat from the pork cut you buy!

❀ Cured Pork of Good Quality: What to Look for

The color of the lean should be a healthy shade of pink. There should be a nice layer of exterior fat and a good amount of marbling. The grain of the muscle should be fine. The iridescent sheen often seen on ham is caused by the breaking up of light by the tiny meat fibers, each fiber having a thin coating of fat.

Since cured products such as ham and bacon are sold under various brand names—each name signifying a certain grade of quality—it is good to acquaint yourself with the meaning of the packing-house brand names in your area. Most large packing houses have from two to three names for grades of ham and from two to seven similar names for grades of bacon. Ask your meat cutter for guidance.

❀ How Pork Is Cut

Unlike beef, veal, and lamb, pork is almost always divided into small cuts at the packing house, for only a portion of the carcass leaves the packing house as fresh pork, the amount de-

PORK CUT CHART

Retail Cuts

Wholesale Cuts

Retail Cuts

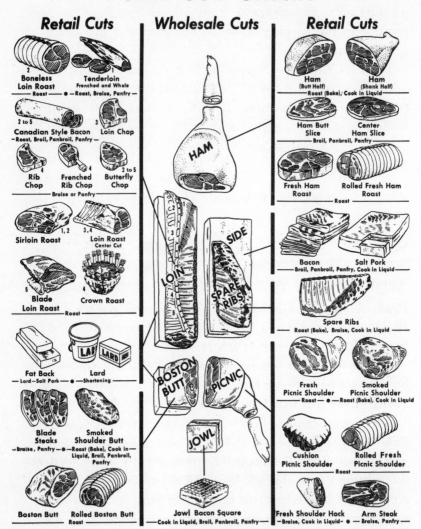

Boneless Loin Roast — 2
Tenderloin Frenched and Whole — 1
— Roast — ● — Roast, Braise, Panfry —

Canadian Style Bacon — 2 to 5
— Roast, Broil, Panbroil, Panfry —
Loin Chop — 3

Rib Chop
Frenched Rib Chop — 4
Butterfly Chop — 2 to 5
— Braise or Panfry —

Sirloin Roast — 1, 2
Loin Roast Center Cut — 3, 4

Blade Loin Roast — 5
Crown Roast — 4
— Roast —

Fat Back
Lard
— Lard—Salt Pork — ● — Shortening —

Blade Steaks
Smoked Shoulder Butt
— Braise, Panfry — ● — Roast (Bake), Cook in Liquid, Broil, Panbroil, Panfry —

Boston Butt
Rolled Boston Butt
— Roast —

HAM

LOIN

SIDE

SPARE RIBS

BOSTON BUTT

PICNIC

JOWL

Jowl Bacon Square
— Cook in Liquid, Broil, Panbroil, Panfry —

Ham (Butt Half)
Ham (Shank Half)
— Roast (Bake), Cook in Liquid —

Ham Butt Slice
Center Ham Slice
— Broil, Panbroil, Panfry —

Fresh Ham Roast
Rolled Fresh Ham Roast
— Roast —

Bacon
Salt Pork
— Broil, Panbroil, Panfry, Cook in Liquid —

Spare Ribs
— Roast (Bake), Braise, Cook in Liquid —

Fresh Picnic Shoulder
Smoked Picnic Shoulder
— Roast — ● — Roast (Bake), Cook in Liquid —

Cushion Picnic Shoulder
Rolled Fresh Picnic Shoulder
— Roast —

Fresh Shoulder Hock
Arm Steak
— Braise, Cook in Liquid — ● — Braise, Panfry —

NATIONAL LIVE STOCK AND MEAT BOARD

pending on market demand. A certain percentage of the meat remains in the packing house to be cured and the fat to be rendered into lard.

The Pork Cut Chart, opposite, shows the usual pork wholesale cuts, although many of the retail cuts also originate in the packing house—for example, sliced bacon, ham, picnic shoulder, tenderloin, Canadian-style bacon.

FRESH PORK

HAM—Wholesale Cut

This cut contains what corresponds roughly to the hind shank, the round, the rump, and the sirloin tip of beef (see Beef Cut Chart). The tail bone is removed. The ham is surrounded by a layer of fat under the rind, or skin.

Ham. A whole fresh ham weighs about 12 pounds and is almost the same cut as a whole beef round except that the tail bone has been removed. It is a large piece of meat and is not too often found on the retail market. The rind can be kept on the ham or it can be removed. When it is removed, some of the excess fat goes with it.

A fresh ham can also be divided into smaller cuts, as in cured ham (see photographs, pp. 256-7). These cuts are called the butt half (upper half), the shank half (lower half), and the shank (containing the hind-shank bones). You may also buy the butt, a cut from the foremost part of the butt half which will contain mostly pelvic bone and not much of the leg bone. A fresh ham may be boned and rolled (see Pork Cut Chart).

To cook: All of these cuts can be roasted. The cooking time depends on the size of the cut—the larger the cut, the less cooking time per pound. For a whole fresh ham count 30 to 35 minutes per pound; for the smaller cuts or a rolled roast count 40 to 45 minutes per pound. All fresh ham should be roasted in a 350° oven and the final thermometer reading should be 185°. Fresh pork is done when none of the meat is the least bit pink. Pork should always be well done.

The rind on the cut need not necessarily be peeled off; score it before cooking and rub salt and pepper into the scoring. The rind when cooked is flavorful and crisp.

There are three herbs that enhance pork especially well. They may be used separately or, in moderation, together: ground thyme, finely crushed bay leaf, and little slips of garlic. For a medium sized roast, use about ⅓ to ½ teaspoon of dried thyme, a bay leaf, and one clove of garlic. Rub the thyme and bay leaf into the fat along with the salt and pepper; use a pointed knife to insert the slips of garlic into the lean. Or use the spicier Dry Marinade for Pork (see Index).

To my mind, sweet things, such as applesauce and sweet potatoes, don't mix with pork that has been seasoned with herbs or garlic. Robert, Pork, or Mustard Sauce (see Index), served in a sauceboat is much better. Save the applesauce and sweet potatoes for cured pork such as smoked ham.

LOIN—Wholesale Cut

This cut corresponds to the sirloin, short loin, and rib of beef (see Beef Cut Chart). As you can see on the Pork Bone Chart, this cut contains part of the bladebone, the backbone, the upper part of the ribs, and the hipbone.

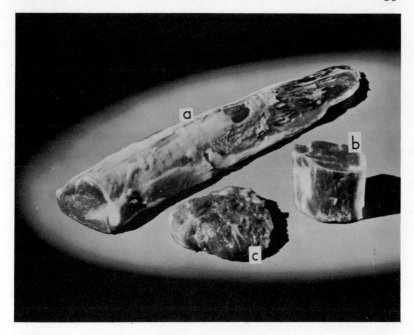

TENDERLOIN

The pork tenderloin is comparable to the tenderloin muscle of beef, but it weighs only ½ to 1 pound. This extremely tender muscle originates in the sirloin section and tapers to an end where the ribs begin. (a) The whole muscle with some of the surrounding fat removed. (b) A slice of the muscle. (c) A flattened slice (this is done with a blow of the flat side of a meat cleaver). The pork tenderloin is usually an expensive cut, but there is no waste in it.

To cook: The tenderloin can be roasted whole. Season it with salt, pepper, and herbs; place in an open pan, lay strips of bacon over the top, and roast in a 350° oven for 35 minutes per pound, or until the meat thermometer reads 185°. It can also be stuffed.

Split it lengthwise, flatten a bit, rub the inside with butter, spread it with about 1 cup of stuffing (see Index), tie it closed, and proceed as you would for a plain roasted tenderloin.

Slices, cut about 1½ inches thick and flattened, can be sautéed slowly in a little oil or butter. They may be seasoned and dredged with flour first, and a little sweet or sour cream may be mixed with the juices left in the pan after cooking and poured over the slices. Count on at least 30 minutes to cook them well.

A whole or part of a tenderloin may also be braised in sweet or sour cream. The meat should be seasoned, dredged with flour, and browned in a little hot fat, butter, or oil. Add about ½ cup of cream, cover the pan, reduce the heat, and cook slowly for about 30 minutes. Mushrooms sautéed in butter make a nice addition.

Sirloin Roast. The face of the roast shown is next to the ham end. The other end will look like a center-cut loin roast (see p. 242). Be sure to look at both ends so as not to mistake it for a center-cut roast. (a) Cross section of the hipbone. (b) The start of the tenderloin muscle. Part of the backbone is in this cut too, and the presence of a good amount of bone makes it difficult to carve. This cut can also be made into chops, and they will somewhat resemble beef sirloin steaks.

Prepare to roast a sirloin cut as you would a fresh ham. Cooking time will be 45 to 50 minutes per pound and the meat thermometer should read 185°.

Boneless Sirloin Roast. This is the same cut as above, but without bones and rolled—a much better way to buy a sirloin cut. Because it is rolled, count on about 50 minutes per pound for roasting.

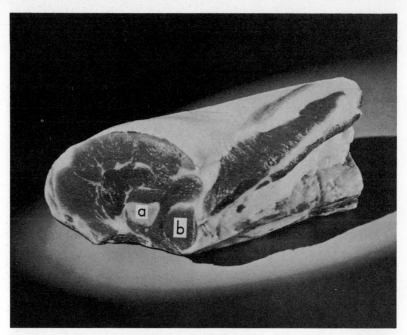

SIRLOIN ROAST

BONELESS SIRLOIN ROAST

LOIN ROAST (center cut)

The choice pork roast. The cut shown in the photograph is large. Portions are often cut off this cut and sold as small loin roasts. When buying a smaller roast, you should look for one with a portion of the tenderloin (c) in it, or next best, the cut comparable to a beef rib roast. When purchasing the latter cut, ask the meat dealer to loosen the backbone from the ribs. Carving will be easier if the backbone is removed after roasting. (a) The backbone with the finger bone extending into the roast. (b) The "eye" muscle. (d) The ribs (you will note in the Pork Bone Chart that pigs have fourteen instead of thirteen ribs).

This center cut will take about 35 to 40 minutes per pound to roast, with smaller roasts taking slightly longer. Prepare and roast as you would a fresh ham.

It should be noted here that a complete loin—a cut extending all the way from the ham to a little past the bladebone—will cook in about 15 to 20 minutes per pound. A whole loin, however, may not fit into a normal-sized oven.

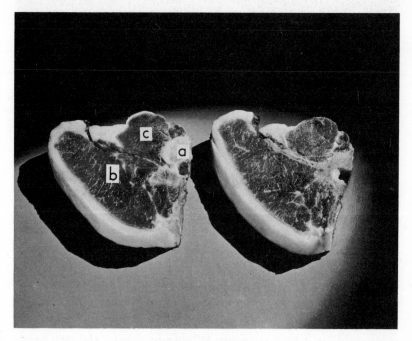

LOIN CHOPS

The choice pork chops. As above, (a) the T-shaped backbone with the finger bone extending into the chop. (b) The "eye" muscle. (c) The tenderloin muscle. These chops are generally cut about ½ inch thick, but you may request thicker ones. They may be sautéed or braised.

To sauté: Use just a tiny bit of fat in a heavy-bottomed skillet;

brown the chops fairly quickly on both sides, salt and pepper each side, reduce the heat, cover the skillet, and cook on the top of the stove or in a 325° oven. Cooking time will be 45 minutes to an hour. Turn the chops every so often to get an even color and, if you are cooking in the oven, when three quarters of the cooking time is up. The chops may be dredged with flour or breaded if you wish; use a bit more fat in the skillet in this case.

To braise: Season the chops and brown them fairly slowly in a little fat for about 10 to 15 minutes per side. Add a little liquid —water, bouillon, tomato juice, apple cider, or sour cream— cover the skillet, reduce the heat, and cook over low heat on top of the stove or in a 325° oven for 30 to 35 minutes.

There are innumerable delicious variations for serving pork chops. May I suggest again serving them with a sauce? Robert, Pork, Lyonnaise, or Mustard Sauce (see Index) will do nicely.

Crown Roast. Made the same way as a lamb crown roast (p. 212), with a sufficient number of ribs to form the circle. Cover the rib ends with cubes of salt pork or raw potato, or wrap them with aluminum foil, to protect them from the heat. Fill the center with stuffing (see Index) if you wish. Since the roast will take a few hours of cooking (35 to 40 minutes per pound in a 350° oven), it is a good idea to keep the center in shape with a Pyrex or metal bowl until one hour before the roast is done and at this time to stuff the center. The stuffing will not dry out if you do this.

If you do not put stuffing in the middle, keep a bowl in the center for the entire cooking time. Season the roast as you would a fresh ham or loin roast, and fill the empty center with potatoes or a vegetable after the roast is cooked.

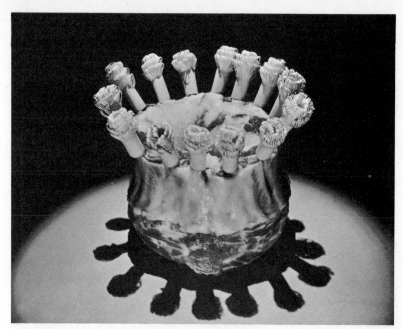

CROWN ROAST

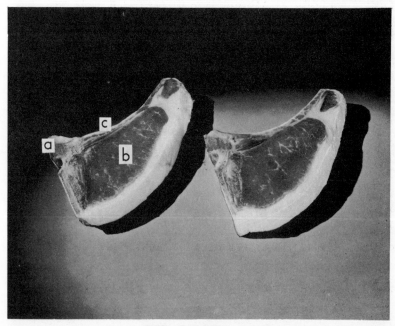

RIB CHOPS

Rib Chops. Cut thick, each chop will contain a rib (c); or every other chop will contain a rib if they are cut thin. (a) The backbone. (b) The rib "eye" muscle. Cook rib chops as you would cook loin chops, allowing 45 minutes to an hour cooking time. Thick rib chops—an inch thick or more—may be stuffed. Cut a pocket in the chop from the *rib* side (remove the rib entirely if necessary). Fill the pocket with stuffing (see Index) and sew or skewer the opening. Brown the chops quickly in a little hot fat, add a small amount of sweet or sour cream, cover, and braise in a 350° oven for an hour. Uncover the pan during the last 10 to 15 minutes for additional browning.

BLADE LOIN ROAST

This is from the end of the loin nearest the shoulder. The cut contains part of the bladebone, backbone, and ribs. It is a less desirable cut because it contains no tenderloin muscle and, because of the various bones, it is more difficult to carve. Prepare and roast this cut as you would fresh ham or any loin roast, counting on 45 to 50 minutes per pound cooking time.

BOSTON BUTT—Wholesale Cut

This cut is what would be the upper part of a beef chuck (see Beef Cut Chart). It contains the shoulder blade; see the Pork Bone Chart. Backbone and neck bone have been removed.

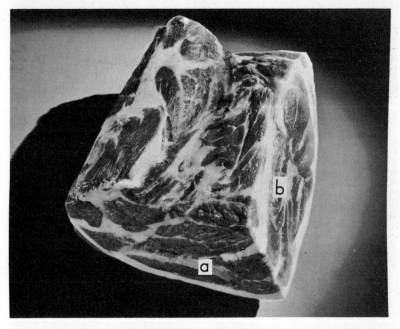

BOSTON BUTT

The wholesale cut minus a certain amount of fat trimmed from the exterior. (a) A cross section of the bladebone near its broadest part. (b) The bladebone again, this time near the knuckle where it joins the arm bone. Although this cut has various muscles, all running in different directions, it can be roasted. The good amount of fat between the muscles makes it a flavorful cut. Roast as you would a fresh ham. Cooking time will be about 45 to 50 minutes per pound.

Sometimes the cut is boned, in which case it is a little easier to carve.

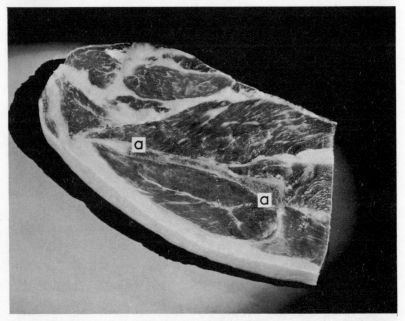

BLADE STEAK

Blade steaks are slices from the Boston butt. (a) The bladebone. The steak in the photograph is one of the first slices from the cut; slices farther up the shoulder will show the bladebone with the ridge. Cook a steak as you would a chop. You may substitute steaks for chops in any recipe except, perhaps, stuffed chops.

PICNIC SHOULDER—*Wholesale Cut*

This is the cut below the Boston butt, or the lower part of the shoulder. It includes the foreleg but not the foot. The bones in this cut are: arm, elbow, and shank.

FRESH PICNIC SHOULDER

This cut is similar to the wholesale cut except that the lower portion of the foreleg may be removed to make a retail cut called hocks. (a) A cross section of the arm bone. (b) The beginning of the foreleg. This cut can be boned and rolled, in which case it is called a rolled picnic shoulder (see Pork Cut Chart). It is wise to buy the cut prepared this way if you plan to carve it before an audience.

The arm section of the shoulder is also cut as an arm roast with the bone still in it, or it can be boned and a pocket made for stuffing, as in lamb cushion shoulder (see p. 215). Ask your meat cutter to leave one side unsewed so that you can put the stuffing in.

Prepare and cook all these cuts as you would a fresh ham. Cooking time will vary a little depending on the type of roast: A picnic shoulder with the bones intact will cook in about 30 to 35 minutes per pound; an arm roast, being smaller, may take about 35 to 40 minutes per pound; a rolled shoulder will take about 40 to 45 minutes per pound; and a cushion shoulder will take from 35 to 40 minutes per pound cooking time. In any case, make sure that the meat thermometer reads 185°.

ARM STEAK

Arm Steak. A cross-sectional slice of the arm. The muscle formation in this cut is different from that of a slice from the
ham, and you can differentiate between the two cuts by noticing
that an arm steak is rounded at one end and flat, or squared,
at the other. (a) The arm bone.

Cook the steak as you would a chop, and, as with the blade
steak from the butt, you may substitute an arm steak in most
recipes that call for chops.

HOCKS

The lower part of the foreleg containing the foreshank bones.
The skin is usually left on the hocks and you should leave it on
when you cook them so the meat will not separate from the
bones. The best way to cook hocks is to simmer them, either in

salted (½ teaspoon per quart) water or a mixture of water and sauerkraut juice, if you plan to serve sauerkraut with them. Cooking time should be 3 to 4 hours.

Serve the hocks with sauerkraut, any of the sauces good for a fresh pork roast or chops, or with Horseradish Sauce (see Index).

Pigs' Feet. The foot is easily recognized. Many consider pigs' feet a delicacy, but don't try them on friends whose tastes you are not sure of! They have a lot of bone and little meat, so you should count on one foot per person.

Be sure the feet are clean; scrub thoroughly and rinse under cold running water. Simmer the feet as you would the hocks; the cooking time will be the same. Bay leaf, a pinch of thyme, and a branch of parsley may be added to the water. Serve with sauerkraut or cabbage.

Spareribs. Wholesale and retail cuts are the same. The cut contains the lower portion of the ribs and the breastbone. As you can see in the Pork Cut Chart, what remains after the spareribs have been removed is the side—the cut that yields bacon and salt pork. (a) The breastbone runs along here. (b) The first seven ribs are attached to the breastbone by the rib cartilages (see the Pork Bone Chart). (c) This flap is the hog's diaphragm.

Barbecued, roasted, simmered—spareribs have an excellent flavor because of the generous amount of fat mingled with the lean. And, besides, they're fun to eat! Fingers allowed. Because of the large portion of bone in this cut, you should count on at least one pound per person.

Spareribs roast in 30 to 35 minutes per pound. Braising will take about 1½ hours, and simmering time should be 30 minutes per pound.

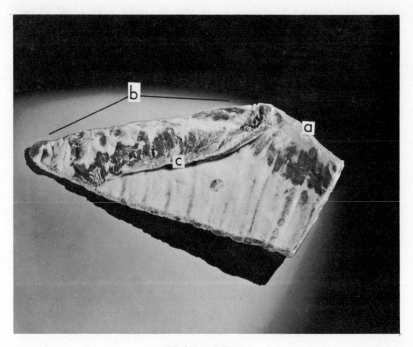

SPARERIBS

You may roast spareribs simply by seasoning them with salt, pepper, a little thyme and part of a crushed bay leaf, and placing them in an oiled baking dish or pan. The oven should be set at 350°. Sauerkraut (1 quart, drained, per 3 pounds of meat) and slices of onion as a bed for the spareribs make a nice variation. Or you may spread one slab of spareribs with a stuffing and cover this with another slab, holding the stuffing in by tying the slabs together (cooking time will be about 1½ hours). If you roast them with a barbecue sauce, be sure to baste frequently.

The internal organs and glands of hogs are usually the least desirable of all the food animals. The liver and kidneys are fairly strong in flavor. The pork heart, however, is a little more tender than that of beef. Hogs yield no sweetbreads because of the age at which they are slaughtered. In general, prepare these pork cuts as you would similar beef cuts (see pp. 129-130 and Index).

GROUND PORK

Ground pork is usually fatter than other ground meats. You can make your own sausage meat with it or use it with other ground meat for meat loaf or stuffing (see Index).

With a little experimentation you can easily arrive at a good formula for fresh sausage that will be as good or better than the all-pork sausage you can buy. Usually the spices and herbs that you add are salt, pepper (freshly ground is best), thyme or sage, and ground bay leaf. Try about ½ teaspoon of salt per pound and go very easy on the herbs and spices, starting with a tiny pinch, until you reach the flavor that pleases you. Be sure to cook a sample thoroughly before you test it for flavor. Shape the mixture into a roll, if you like, and cover it well with waxed paper. Do not store in the refrigerator longer than three days, and remember, also, that sausage meat does not freeze well.

Some meat markets grind pork and add their own formula of seasonings; the quantity and type of seasonings can very widely from market to market.

CURED PORK

Pork is by far the most often cured meat in this country. A good percentage of every slaughtered hog remains at the packing house to be cured or cured and smoked. Curing is one of the oldest forms of meat preservation. Originally, salt was simply rubbed into the meat (this is called the dry-salt method) or the meat was packed in barrels of salt (this is how the meat "packer" got his name). It was then discovered that by keeping the meat in a "pickle" or brine—composed of such ingredients as salt, sugar, saltpeter, pepper (sometimes), and water—a more satisfactory product could be obtained. The salt is the main preserving agent; sugar improves the flavor and counteracts some of the dryness and hardness produced by salt alone. Saltpeter (sodium nitrate) acts as a preservative and gives the meat its pink color. Pepper is added for flavoring and some preservation purposes. A brine to which sugar has been added is called a sweet pickle. The dry-salt method, however, is still used on some cuts of pork, salt pork, for example.

Meat is smoked to help in its preservation and to improve its flavor. Smoke from hard woods, such as hickory and maple, produces the best results.

Today the packing houses carefully guard their secrets of curing and smoking. Formulas are precise and the processes are rigidly controlled. In former days all curing was done in vats. Now new techniques are continually being worked on. Fairly recent methods used in curing are to inject the pickle into the meat with multiple needles resembling hypodermic needles or to pump the pickle in through the arteries.

Cured and smoked meats produced by packing houses are:

Ham. A whole cured ham corresponds to a whole fresh ham. In the photographs (see next pages) it has been cut in half, forming the shank and butt ends (see fresh ham, p. 237, for further explanation of these cuts). A whole ham weighs anywhere from 8 to 18

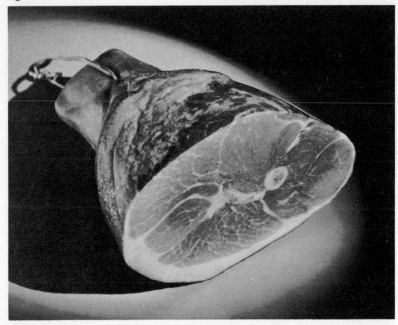

HALF HAM (shank end)

pounds, 8 to 10 pounds being small, 10 to 15 pounds being medium, and 15 to 18 pounds being large. A half ham will usually weigh 5 to 8 pounds.

Hams have many variations: There is the so-called country ham or aged ham. It is cured and smoked now in much the same way it has been for the past two hundred years. The preserving process is a slow one—the hams are hung at least a year —and the exterior may even be a little moldy by the time the ham is thoroughly cured. Virginia, Smithfield, and Kentucky hams are aged hams (sometimes called country-cured hams) that have received a special cure.

Most hams produced by national packing houses these days have received what is called a mild cure. They can be bought

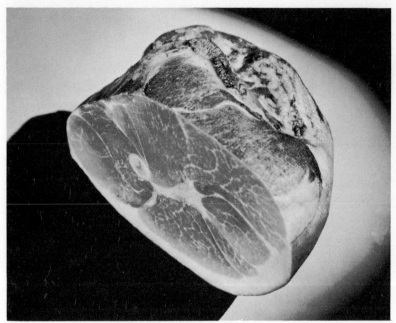

HALF HAM (butt end)

either uncooked (actually they are already partially tenderized) or fully cooked (precooked). There may be a local packing house in your community that makes hams by this method. Often it will use a special kind of wood for smoke which gives the hams a distinctive flavor. Hams may also be purchased canned. Most canned hams are thoroughly cooked and need only to be heated. These hams are perishable and should be stored in the refrigerator even while they are in the can. Be sure to read the label on a canned ham carefully; it will give you storing and cooking instructions. Canned hams come from Europe as well as United States; many European hams have a slightly different flavor—due to a difference in curing—from the American hams.

Frequently hams are wrapped and labeled, the label often including cooking instructions. Be sure to follow these basic instructions. Below I shall give general cooking guides to use if you buy a ham without accompanying cooking instructions. Whenever you are in doubt about the condition of a ham—whether or not it has been precooked, etc.—be sure to ask your meat dealer.

To bake an uncooked, mild-cure smoked ham: Unlike an aged ham, these hams need no soaking or boiling. If the ham you buy comes specially wrapped, remove both wrappers, saving the inside one. Wipe the ham with a damp cloth, do not remove the rind, and then rewrap it loosely in the inside wrapper (or aluminum foil instead, if you wish). Insert a meat thermometer into the thickest part of the ham, through the wrapping, and do not let the bulb rest on the bone. Place the ham, fat side up, on a rack in a roasting pan. Have your oven set at 300°. A large ham will bake (roast) in from 15 to 18 minutes per pound, a medium ham in from 18 to 22 minutes per pound, a small ham in from 22 to 25 minutes per pound, and a half ham in from 25 to 30 minutes per pound. The meat thermometer should read 165° when the ham is done. When the ham is cooked, remove it from the oven and cut off the rind with a sharp knife or kitchen scissors, leaving a small collar of rind around the shank bone for carving and appearance's sake. Score the fat with a knife and glaze the ham, if you wish. Return the glazed ham to a 400° oven for about 15 minutes. This hot temperature at the last gives the ham an attractive surface.

To glaze: There are numerous glazes that are good on ham. One of my favorites, enough for a whole ham, is: 1 cup of brown sugar mixed with 1 teaspoon dry mustard, ½ teaspoon of ground cloves, and enough pineapple juice, cider, Madeira, or sherry to make a paste that can be spread over the ham.

To bake a precooked, mild-cure smoked ham: These hams often come with the bone removed. But bone in or out, if you want to eat the ham hot, simply place it, fat side up, on a rack in an open roasting pan and bake it for 15 to 20 minutes per pound in a 325° oven. The meat thermometer should read 130° when the ham is thoroughly hot. You may glaze a cooked ham as you would an uncooked ham, replacing it in a 400° oven for about 15 minutes to set the glaze.

To cook a country-cured ham, or a Virginia- or Kentucky-style ham, etc.: These hams have a rich reddish-brown exterior. They should be thoroughly scrubbed with soap and water and a brush to remove any mold. Be sure to rinse the soap off well with hot water. Soak the ham in cold water to cover at least overnight (or up to two days) if it is a few years old. Drain, and simmer in fresh water to cover for 30 minutes per pound. Allow it to cool in the simmer water, then cut off the rind, score the fat, glaze, and bake in a 350° oven for 45 minutes to an hour.

HAM SLICE

A ham slice will somewhat resemble a beef round steak (p. 98). It will contain a cross section of the round bone and it will be oval in shape. You can often buy the slices already cut, or you can ask your meat cutter to cut you a slice of any thickness you want. Thickness for a slice of ham may vary anywhere from ½ inch to 1 inch, or you can request a slice to be cut up to about 2 inches thick. Sliced ham can come from anywhere on the leg, but it is usually cut from somewhere near the dividing line between the shank and butt ends. These slices are called center cuts.

The thinner slices (up to 1 inch) can be broiled or panbroiled.

Cooking time depends on thickness and whether the ham is uncooked or precooked.

Panbroiling: Cut the fat around the edge at intervals to prevent curling. Rub a little ham fat in a fairly hot pan. Brown the slice in it over a moderate heat; turn once. A ¼-inch slice will cook in 5 to 6 minutes, a ½-inch slice in 8 to 10 minutes, a ¾-inch slice in 12 to 14 minutes, and a 1-inch slice in 15 to 16 minutes. If the slice is precooked, reduce cooking time by 2 minutes.

Broiling: Cut the fat around the edge at intervals to prevent curling. Have broiler temperature moderately hot (400° to 450°) and leave a 3-inch space between the meat and the heat. Cut broiling times below in half if ham is precooked:

Thickness	Minutes per Side
⅓ inch	3-4
½ inch	5-6
¾ inch	7-8
1 inch	10-12

Thicker slices of ham (over 1 inch) are best baked, and they are usually baked in liquid. You may also glaze the top of the slice before baking (see glaze recipe, p. 258). The liquid may be milk, broth in which the ham has previously simmered, cider or apple juice, other fruit juice, or wine (Madeira or sweet sherry). Use ½ to 1 cup of liquid, depending upon the size of the slice. You may cook it covered or uncovered, in a 350° oven. If you cover the pan, remove the cover for the last 10 to 15 minutes. Cooking time for uncooked ham should be an hour per inch. A precooked ham slice will bake in about one-third to one-half that time. If the slice is from an aged ham, simmer it in water before baking. Simmering time should be half an hour.

CANADIAN-STYLE BACON

This bacon is the "eye" muscle running along the back (the large muscle in pork chops; see Pork Cut Chart) that has been cured and smoked. It usually comes in a casing of some sort. It is an excellent substitute for ham if your family is small or if you want just one meal's worth of smoked pork.

You may bake Canadian-style bacon and serve it as you would a ham. Score and glaze. Bake in a 350° oven for about 25 minutes per pound. Thermometer reading should be 160°. It may dry out while baking, so it is a good idea to baste it a few times with fruit juice, cider, or wine (Madeira or sweet sherry).

Slices of this bacon can be panbroiled. Rub the pan with a little butter first because there is not much fat in Canadian-style bacon. Cook over low heat as you would regular bacon, turning it frequently. Cooking time will be 5 to 10 minutes, depending on the thickness of the slice.

Bacon. Sliced bacon comes either thick-sliced, regular, or thin-sliced, and it has been packaged at the packing house. Sliced bacon tends to become rancid fairly quickly. You may get fresher bacon, or have it cut a particular thickness, if you ask your meat cutter to cut the amount you want off an unsliced slab. Or you can buy any amount of a slab and slice it yourself. As you can see on the Pork Cut Chart, bacon comes from the side after the spareribs have been removed.

Most packaged bacon has accompanying cooking instructions for panbroiling, broiling, or baking. If you find yourself without instructions, you may follow these:

Panbroiling: Place the strips in a cold skillet and cook over low heat until the desired degree of doneness is reached. This will take from 5 to 7 minutes unless you are cooking thick-sliced bacon. Turn the bacon as many times as you want, although usually one or twice is sufficient. For crispness, pour off the fat as it accumulates. Drain the bacon on paper toweling.

Broiling: Have the broiler at medium heat and place the bacon on a rack about 3 to 4 inches from the heat. Turn once during the cooking. Cooking time will be 2 to 3 minutes per side, depending on thickness. Drain on absorbent paper if necessary.

Baking: Place bacon on a wire rack in a dripping pan and bake in a preheated 400° oven until the bacon is crisp. Cooking time will be around 10 minutes. It is not absolutely necessary to separate the slices at first if you use this method, and it's a good way to cook large amounts—a one-pound package, for instance.

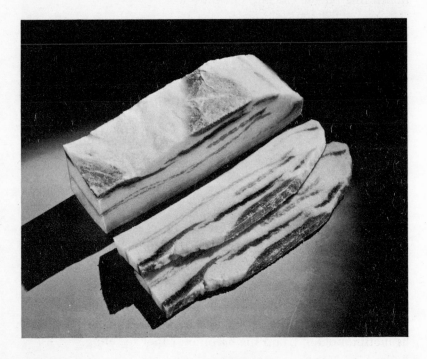

SALT PORK

Salt pork also comes from the side. It generally contains less lean than bacon. It has been cured by the dry salt method and has not been smoked. Salt pork is used for larding and barding purposes (see Chapter 7), and for flavoring and adding fat to many dishes—baked beans, clam chowder, etc. You can usually buy it in small quantities from your meat market. It is more desirable to use salt pork for larding purposes than bacon, as it does not have the smoked flavor.

SMOKED SHOULDER BUTT

Sometimes called a cottage roll, this is the "eye" of the Boston butt. It has been mild-cured and smoked in the same way as ham. It somewhat resembles Canadian-style bacon, but it will have more intermingled fat and the grain will be coarser. Like Canadian-style bacon, it can replace ham for a small family. The rolls usually weigh from 1 to 4 pounds each.

Since the shoulder butt is rolled at the packing house, cooking instructions will usually be on the wrapping. This roll can be baked or simmered, the latter method being the more de-desirable because there is a certain amount of thick connective tissue present.

To cook: Bake a smoked shoulder butt in a 300° oven for 35 to 40 minutes per pound. The meat thermometer should read 170°. You may score and glaze it (see glaze recipe, p. 258). Baste during the baking period if the meat should look dry.

Or simmer this cut in water, adding such flavorings as bay leaf, a clove of garlic, a few cloves, and a few peppercorns. Simmering time will be about 35 to 45 minutes per pound, or until the meat is tender.

Slices of this cut can be panbroiled like Canadian-style bacon.

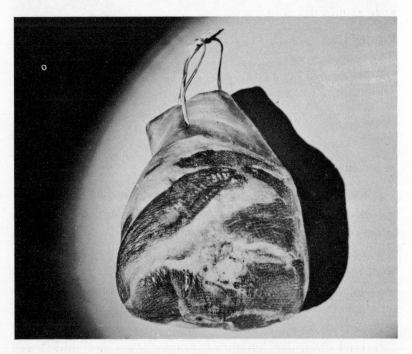

SMOKED PICNIC SHOULDER

See fresh picnic shoulder, p. 249, for a description of the cut. A "picnic" has been cured and smoked in the same way as ham.

There is a good deal more fat, bone, and tough connective tissue in it than in ham, and the grain of the lean is coarser—hence the usually lower cost.

To cook: You can bake a picnic shoulder as you would a ham. Cooking time will be 35 minutes per pound and the thermometer should read 170° when the meat is cooked. The better way to cook it, however, is to simmer it in water, adding 1 or 2 cloves of garlic, a bay leaf, 6 to 8 peppercorns, 1 to 2 stalks of celery cut into large slices, and a few cloves. Simmering time will be 35 to 45 minutes per pound.

Pickled Pigs' Feet. These feet are usually found in jars, still in their pickle juice. They are completely cooked, ready to eat, and delicious if the anatomy doesn't bother you! They are eaten cold and are good with cole slaw or potato salad, dark bread, and beer for a light evening supper on a hot day.

A Word about Sausages

It seems to me fitting that a section on sausage should follow the information on cured and smoked pork because so many sausages are cured and smoked also. Although there are all-pork sausages, most sausages are a mixture of pork and beef, or pork, beef, and veal, plus seasonings. There are hundreds of varieties of sausage in this country because so many nationalities have settled here, bringing with them their recipes and particular sausage preferences. I am not going to attempt to tell you about each kind (even the thought of it overwhelms me!), and I will mainly concern myself here with some sausages familiar in America.

Sausages are divided into two large groups—fresh and dry—

and both of these large groups contain smaller ones. Fresh sausages should be kept in the refrigerator and should be cooked and eaten within a few days of purchase. Their flavor is usually milder than that of most of the dry sausages. None of the dry sausages requires cooking. Practically all sausage comes in casings made from meat-animal intestines, though additional synthetic casings (which should be removed after slicing) are becoming common on some sausages.

FRESH SAUSAGES

The most common fresh sausages, which you have to cook thoroughly, are all-pork sausage, smoked fresh sausage or country sausage, and bockwurst.

All-Pork Sausage. This sausage (also called pure pork sausage) comes in links, patties, or bulk (sausage meat). It is seasoned with spices and herbs, and you will find some variation in its flavor due to the different amounts of spices and herbs used by the manufacturers. Links are best cooked when they are simmered first (covered) for about 5 minutes in a small amount (about 2 tablespoons) of water. The cover is then removed and the links should cook slowly until brown. They should be turned with a spoon, not pierced with a fork. Pour off any extra water or fat. Cooking time will be 10 to 15 minutes. Patties, whether you buy them already made or make them yourself from bulk sausage, should be started in a cold skillet. Brown them slowly for about 15 minutes, turning them so they are well browned on both sides.

Smoked Fresh Sausage or Country Sausage. Often this sausage will contain some ground beef or veal. The pork is more coarsely ground in these sausages and they most often come in links or in an unlinked casing. Cook as you would all-pork sausage.

Bockwurst. These chubby white sausages flecked with tiny spots of green (chives and parsley) are usually only made in the spring. A couple of bockwursts, a glass of bock beer, and some good dark bread always mean mild weather is here at last, and it's my way of celebrating the new season every year.

Beef, veal, and pork—ground very fine, mixed together with eggs, milk, seasonings, chives, and parsley, and all stuffed in a casing—make these rather delicately flavored sausages. Since they are neither precooked nor smoked, they are highly perishable and, as any freshly ground meat, should be cooked almost immediately after purchase.

You may cook them as you would fresh pork sausage, starting with a small amount of water in a covered skillet. Or, in the German way, cover them with water, bring to the boiling point, then lower the heat and simmer them very gently for 10 minutes. (If the water continues to boil, the bockwursts will split.) Eat them plain with a glass of bock beer or serve them as you would fresh pork sausage.

Swiss Sausage. Something like a bockwurst, this sausage should also be thoroughly cooked.

Other Fresh Sausages. Classed under fresh sausage, also, is the frankfurter, which is a combination of beef and pork (unless otherwise stated on the label). It has been smoked and cooked, and among its variations are: knackwurst (flavored with garlic); Viennawurst (tiny frankfurters cut at either end); and kolbassy (a polish sausage highly flavored with garlic and other seasonings). A bologna sausage is somewhat like a glorified frankfurter. It too has been smoked and cooked, but it can vary quite a bit in flavor depending on the maker of the sausage. Bologna is made of finely ground beef, pork, and sometimes veal, with mild seasonings.

Another fresh sausage is liver sausage and its variations: liverwurst (finely ground pork, liver, and seasonings); Braunschweiger (smoked liver sausage often made with milk and eggs); and Strassburg (liver sausage that has veal and pistachio nuts added).

A third class of fresh sausage is blood sausage. It also has many variations: biroldo, blutwurst, and Thuringer blood sausage are three such.

Other fresh sausages include headcheese (small pieces of cooked pork head meat and sometimes pork tongue held together by gelatin); Italian hot sausage (coarsely cut cured pork and finely cut beef, with fennel and wine among the seasonings); and mettwurst—German for "meat sausage" (very finely ground beef or pork, or a combination of the two, put in casings, cured, and smoked, it is often used as a spread for sandwiches or appetizers).

Since all the fresh sausage listed above (with, of course, the exception of the all-pork sausages and bockwurst) have been cooked and possibly smoked, they need no further cooking. But some of these sausages are best when heated, namely, those of the frankfurter family. To heat these, simmer in water to cover for about 7 minutes if they are stout or for about 5 minutes if they are slim. Frankfurters may also be split and broiled, or baked in casserole dishes.

DRY SAUSAGES

Dry sausages are often called summer sausages because at one time they were mainly sold in the summer. They keep well, even at a moderately warm temperature. These sausages have been cured and some are smoked—sometimes for several days. Other sausages have been cured and hung in drying rooms for periods up to three months. I shall mention just a few of the more widely known dry sausages:

Salame. Made from a mixture of pork and beef with a variety of seasonings. Salami vary in size and in flavor. Some are smoked; some are air dried. The coarseness of the ground meat varies. Practically every country has its own special salame.

Cervelat: Comparable to salame, but usually less highly seasoned and with the meat more finely ground, cervelat also varies greatly in size. It is smoked after the meat has been stuffed in the casing. Also classed under salame or cervelat are: Thuringer (a cervelat); Italian salame (red wine and garlic are two of its ingredients); salamette (salame made in small links); and Goteborg (Swedish cervelat).

Mortadella. This is a highly seasoned Italian sausage that is made with a combination of finely ground cured pork and beef and cubes of pork fat. It comes in rather large casings and it has been air dried.

Pepperone. Again an Italian sausage. It is highly spiced and contains coarsely ground black pepper. Pork and beef, coarsely ground, are the meats in it. The mixture is cured before it is put in the casings and then air dried. This may sound a bit like going overboard, but I like to eat generous slices of pepperone followed with a good swallow of beer.

Pork Recipes

See Chapter 8 for a number of sauces that are good with pork.

PEASANT PORK ROAST

(For 4)

1 pork loin (rib or loin end), weighing about 4 lbs.
1 large clove garlic
Salt and pepper
3 tablespoons butter
4 potatoes
2 large onions, minced
2 sprigs parsley, chopped

Insert slips of garlic into the meat so that they are evenly distributed over the surface of the roast. Sprinkle the roast generously with salt and pepper; then with your hands rub the seasoning into the meat. Roast the loin in a 350° oven, 35 to 40 minutes per pound, or until the meat thermometer reaches 185°.

Parboil the potatoes for 15 to 20 minutes in their skins, then peel and quarter them. Melt the butter in a skillet and lightly sauté the potatoes in it. Add the minced onions to the potatoes and allow them to just heat in the butter. Forty-five minutes before the roast is done, add the potatoes and onions to the roasting pan, surrounding but not covering the meat.

Serve the roast on a platter, surrounded by the potatoes and onions, which have been sprinkled with parsley.

PORK CHOPS AND CABBAGE

(For 4)

4 large or 8 small pork chops (loin or rib)
Salt and pepper
1 teaspoon bacon drippings
4 tablespoons minced onion
Bouquet garni (bay leaf, sprig of parsley, 1/4 teaspoon dried thyme)
3 tablespoons butter
1 small cabbage, shredded
1/4 cup cream
1 teaspoon white-wine vinegar

Season the chops on both sides with salt and pepper. Melt the bacon drippings in a skillet and brown the chops in them over a medium heat. When the chops are brown, sprinkle the minced onion over them, add the bouquet garni, cover the skillet, and simmer the chops for 35 to 40 minutes.

Meanwhile, melt the 3 tablespoons of butter in a saucepan, and lightly sauté the shredded cabbage in it for about 3 minutes. Cover the pan and complete the cooking over very low heat for 30 minutes. When the cabbage is cooked, mix in the cream and heat but do not allow to boil.

On a hot platter make a mound of the cabbage. In a circular pattern lay the chops on top of it. Discard the bouquet garni. Stir the vinegar with the juices in the chop pan and pour this over the chops before serving.

PORK CHOPS WITH JEAN SAUCE
(For 4)

4 large or 8 small pork chops (loin or rib)
Salt and pepper
1 teaspoon bacon drippings
¼ cup tomato juice
1 small onion, minced
¼ cup dry white wine
½ cup Brown Sauce (see Index)
1 teaspoon dry mustard

Season the chops on both sides with salt and pepper. Melt the bacon drippings in a skillet, and brown the chops in them over medium heat for 10 to 12 minutes per side. Add the tomato juice to the skillet and cover. Simmer for 35 minutes.

When the chops are done, remove them from the skillet and keep them warm. In the fat remaining in the skillet sauté the onion; then remove, by skimming with a spoon, as much of the fat as possible. Add the wine and allow it to boil for 1 to 2 minutes. Add the Brown Sauce, mix well, and simmer for another 1 to 2 minutes. Stir in the mustard; mix but do not boil. Pour the sauce over the chops and serve.

BAKED PORK CHOPS
(For 4)

4 rib pork chops, cut thick
2 tablespoons butter
1 clove garlic, halved lengthwise
⅛ teaspoon dried thyme
½ bay leaf

Bone the chops with a sharp knife. Melt the butter in a thick skillet. Rub the cut sides of the garlic over the bottom of a heavy skillet, then discard all but a sliver of the garlic. Leave the sliver in the pan, add the butter, heat it, and mix in the thyme and bay leaf. Season the chops with salt and pepper, and brown them in the seasoned butter over medium heat. When they are brown, cover the skillet and place it in a 325° oven. After 30 minutes of cooking, remove the cover, turn the chops, and continue cooking uncovered. Turn the chops again after 10 minutes and allow them to cook for another, final 10 minutes.

BARBECUED SPARERIBS
(For 4)

3½ to 4 lbs. spareribs, cut into serving pieces

Barbecue Sauce:

1 large onion, minced
2 tablespoons sesame oil
1 cup catsup
1 tablespoon Worcestershire Sauce
1 tablespoon sugar
Juice 1 lemon
¼ teaspoon Tabasco Sauce
4 tablespoons soy sauce

To be served with:

Sesame seeds
Chinese mustard (dry mustard mixed to a paste with flat beer)

Barbecue Sauce: Sauté the onion in the oil until transparent. Add the other ingredients and mix well. Boil the mixture for 1 minute.

Brush the spareribs with the barbecue sauce and bake in a 350° oven for 1½ hours; or broil them over charcoal very slowly until they are well browned on all sides. Turn the spareribs and baste with the sauce every 20 minutes.

Serve with small individual bowls of sesame seeds and of Chinese mustard. To eat, the spareribs are first dipped into the mustard and then into the sesame seeds.

PORK TENDERLOIN IN SOUR CREAM
(For 4)

1 large or 2 small pork tenderloins
3 tablespoons butter, in all
½ lb. fresh mushrooms, or 6-oz. can mushrooms, coarsely
    chopped
½ clove garlic
Flour
Salt and pepper
¼ teaspoon dried thyme
1 cup sour cream

In a heavy skillet large enough eventually to accommodate the tenderloin, sauté the chopped mushrooms in 2 tablespoons of the butter until they are brown.

Split the tenderloin lengthwise, but do not sever completely, and flatten each side with the side of a heavy knife or cleaver. Rub the inside well with the garlic and spread with the sautéed mushrooms. Sew or tie the tenderloin back together well.

Dredge the tenderloin with flour that has been well seasoned with salt, pepper, and the thyme. Add the remaining tablespoon of butter to the skillet, and brown the meat slowly in it until it is golden. Add the sour cream, cover the skillet and cook in a 325° oven for 35 minutes per pound. Calculate by the weight of one tenderloin only, should you be cooking two of them.

ALSATIAN PORK TENDERLOIN

(For 4)

8 slices of pork tenderloin, cut 1½ inches thick and flattened
Salt and pepper
Flour
3 tablespoons butter, in all
8 very thin slices of onion (as near the diameter of the
    tenderloin slices as possible)
¼ teaspoon dill seeds
½ cup heavy cream or sour cream

Season the tenderloin slices with salt and pepper and dredge them with flour. Brown the slices in 2 tablespoons of the butter over medium heat. When they are a golden brown, remove them from the skillet. Add the remaining tablespoon of butter to the skillet and in it sauté the slices of onion on one side only, being careful not to let the rings separate; remove them when they are golden. Put the tenderloin slices back into the skillet and cover each piece with an onion slice, sautéed side up. Cover and cook over low heat for 15 to 20 minutes. When the meat is done, remove to a hot platter. Add the dill seeds and cream to the skillet. Stir well, heat barely to boiling point, and pour over the meat.

STUFFING FOR PORK TENDERLOIN AND PORK CHOPS

(For 8 chops or one tenderloin)

5 tablespoons butter
1 large onion, finely chopped
½ cup mushrooms (fresh or canned), finely chopped
¼ teaspoon dried thyme
¼ cup chopped parsley
1 cup fine dry bread crumbs
Salt and pepper
1 egg

Sauté the onion in the butter. When it is transparent, add the mushrooms, thyme, parsley, and bread crumbs. Stir over the heat for a minute, then remove the pan from the stove, salt and pepper to taste, and stir in the egg, which has been lightly beaten. Stuff the chops or tenderloin.

DRY MARINADE FOR ROAST PORK

"Marinade" is somewhat of a misnomer for this type of seasoning, as the purpose is only seasoning, not tenderizing as well, as is the case with other marinades. However, it is a flavorful way to treat a roast of pork. You may use it for either boned or unboned roasts, though the herbs will be more effective on a boned cut.

For a roast weighing 2 pounds after boning, crush together to a powder 2 tablespoons of coarse salt, ½ teaspoon of dried thyme, ½ teaspoon of mixed powdered clove, cinnamon, and nutmeg, 1 small bay leaf, and a dozen peppercorns. (This can be done in a wooden bowl with a wooden potato masher, though a mortar and pestle is the ideal tool.) Rub the meat well on all sides and in every crevice with this powder, then roll and tie it if necessary. Let it stand in a cool place for 24 hours before roasting.

HAM WITH A HEAD

1 cooked ham, rind removed
1 can beer
½ to 1 cup sugar, depending on size of ham
½ to 1 teaspoon dry mustard, depending on size of ham

Place the ham in a roasting pan and pour over it ½ to 1 cup of beer, depending on the size of the ham. Roast in a 325° oven for 15 minutes per pound, or until the meat thermometer reaches 130°. Baste with the beer every 15 minutes.

Mix the sugar and mustard together with enough beer to make a paste. Remove the ham from the oven when it is hot, and spread it with the paste. Return to a 400° oven for 15 minutes, or until the ham is well glazed.

Do what you want with the beer remaining in the can!

SAUSAGES AND CABBAGE

(For 4)

1 to 1½ lbs. link sausages
2 tablespoons butter
3 tablespoons flour
1½ cups boiling water
1 medium cabbage, quartered
Bouquet garni (bay leaf, ¼ teaspoon dried thyme, sprig of
    parsley)

Simmer the sausages in 2 tablespoons of water for 5 minutes.
Uncover the pan and continue cooking them slowly. When they
are a golden brown on all sides, remove them from the pan and
pour off all but one tablespoon of the fat. Melt the butter in the
same pan, and add the flour, mixing well. Allow this to brown
slowly for 5 to 10 minutes. Then gradually stir in the boiling
water, and when the mixture is thoroughly blended, add the
bouquet garni. Salt and pepper to taste.

While preparing the sauce, parboil the cabbage quarters in a
small amount of water for 15 minutes. Drain the cabbage well
and add it and the sausages to the sauce. Simmer together, uncovered, for 30 minutes. Remove the bouquet garni. Place the
cabbage in the center of a platter, surround it with the sausages,
and pour the sauce over all.

CHAPTER 14

CHICKEN

Chicken, more than any other poultry or fowl and more than some meats, makes a regular appearance as the meat course on the American dinner table. Thus, I have included it in this meat cookbook.

If I were writing this book not too many years ago I would tell you to look for a clear-eyed, bright-combed and bright-feathered, plump, live chicken. Or, if you preferred the dressed chicken, I would tell you to check for a flexible breastbone (in a young, tender bird you should be able to wiggle it like the end of your nose) and to check the feet to see that they have no large, hard scales.

But the trend in American markets is toward packaging of everything, and poultry is no exception, especially in super-markets, which sell little but packaged chicken, be it in boxes or thoroughly encased in a transparent plastic wrapping. To a certain extent you can see through the window of the box or through the wrapping to check the "finish" of the chicken—the skin should be uniformly light in color—but it is almost im-possible to check such things as the consistency of the skin—it should be soft and pliable—or the flexibility of the breastbone.

If your market carries fresh-killed poultry, unpackaged and presented so that you can really tell what you are getting, you are fortunate; in certain areas this is still at least partly the custom, particularly where poultry is raised locally. In any case, the possible choices are those of fresh whole, drawn and dressed birds; of chicken already cut into serving pieces; of frozen chicken of any size or shape, or also cut in pieces; and very often, also, of birds that have been treated with the antibiotic, chlortetracycline, to retard spoiling. Whatever kind of chicken you buy, when you find the market and the chicken that please you most, stick to them.

Chickens are classified according to age, weight, and sex:

Broilers. Young chickens of either sex whose ages range from 6 to 14 weeks. They weigh between ¾ to 2½ pounds and their meat is tender and fine-textured. As their name implies, they are best suited to broiling, although they are the choice of many cooks for sautéing or roasting. A very small broiler will serve one person; half of a larger broiler is sufficient for one serving. Three fourths to one pound of chicken per person is a good gauge for the amount to buy.

To cook: To broil, split the broiler in half lengthwise with poultry shears, cutting up through the ribs on either side of the backbone. Remove the neck and backbone. Cut out some of the breastbone and break the joints by snapping them. Some poultry dealers do this for their customers. The chicken should lie as flat as possible. Keep it at room temperature for an hour before cooking. Just before broiling, rub it well with butter or oil and season with salt and pepper. Place the chicken in a preheated broiler (375°), skin side down. The uppermost part should be about 3½ to 4 inches from the heat. Cook for 15 to

20 minutes. Turn, brush the skin with more butter or oil, and continue cooking for another 15 to 20 minutes. If it is not done at the end of this time (no pink juice should run from the leg), lower the heat a little, or move the broiler rack farther away from the heat, and continue cooking for a few minutes.

Sauté or roast the broiler as you would a fryer (see below). The cooking time will be a little less.

Fryers. Chickens of either sex whose ages range from 14 to 20 weeks and that weigh from 2½ to 3½ pounds. Because fryers are a little older than broilers, they will be a little more plump. Their meat is tender and fine-grained enough for sautéing, frying, or roasting.

To sauté: The chicken should be divided into quarters, or the larger birds should be divided into serving pieces—legs, thighs, etc. Season the pieces with salt and pepper and lightly dredge with flour if you like. Heat 2 tablespoons of butter, oil, or other fat in a skillet until it is hot but not smoking. Brown the chicken quickly—but don't burn it—in the hot fat. When the pieces are a nice golden color, you may either continue the cooking on the top of the stove over a moderate heat by covering the pan for about 30 minutes and then uncovering it for 10 to 15 minutes to crisp the chicken—or, you may continue cooking it, uncovered, in a 325° oven for about 35 to 45 minutes. If you like your chicken very well done, the cooking time may be longer. Be sure not let it dry out; turn the pieces one or two times. After the chicken is removed, use everything that remains in the pan as the base for a pan sauce.

To fry: There are many ways to fry chicken—variations not only in the actual method of frying but also in what the pieces are covered with before they are fried, such as egg and bread crumbs, or flour, or a batter of some sort. Many recipes for frying chicken are simply variations of the sauté recipe, but they call for about double the amount of fat (pieces covered with batter or the like absorb more fat). Then there are recipes that really do not call for frying at all. The pieces are actually braised, because these recipes call for the addition of liquid.* And, finally, there are the recipes for deep-fat frying—many calling for the pieces to be simmered until partially or completely tender before they are covered with a batter and deep-fat fried. Although I believe all but the first methods listed here actually belong under headings other than that of frying, I shall include them here since "frying" is the word generally used for them and because a "fryer" is the type of bird to which they usually apply.

Various preparations for coating pieces of chicken before frying are listed after these four versions of the frying process:

I. Melt enough fat (use at least part butter for the best flavor) in a skillet to make a depth of at least ½ inch. Cover the pieces of chicken with one of the preparations listed below, and fry them in the fat which has first been heated to a moderately hot temperature. When the pieces are a golden brown, continue the cooking in a 325° oven for 30 to 60 minutes, depending on the size of the chicken. You can cover the skillet and continue the cooking over low heat on the top of the stove, but the exterior

* To add to the confusion in terminology, the French recipe names you often find in cookbooks will use the word "sauté" for this kind of braising. In European recipe parlance, this usage is correct because the recipes begin with a preliminary browning or sautéing of the chicken. See the braising process on p. 288.

crust will be a little soggy. Be sure to turn the pieces once or twice while they are cooking.

II. Melt fat to a depth of at least 1 inch. It should be hot before you add the chicken, which has been covered with one of the preparations listed below. Fry the pieces to a golden brown. You will probably have to fry them a few at a time; put the browned pieces in a large pan as they are done. When all of the pieces have been browned, place the pan in a 200° oven, and continue cooking for about 2 hours.

III. Melt fat to a depth of $\frac{1}{4}$ inch. Cover the chicken with one of the preparations listed below. Brown the pieces fairly slowly in the hot fat. When golden brown, pour over the chicken about $\frac{1}{4}$ cup of liquid—water, chicken stock, or dry white or red wine —and cover the pan tightly. Reduce the heat to a simmer and continue cooking the chicken for 30 to 60 minutes.

IV. Simmer the pieces of chicken for 20 minutes in water to cover to which a few rounds of carrot, half an onion, a few slices of celery, 2 or 3 peppercorns, and $\frac{1}{2}$ teaspoon of salt have been added. Drain, and cover the pieces with one of the preparations listed below. Heat fat at least 2 inches deep to 360°, and deep fry the pieces for 5 to 7 minutes.

COATINGS AND BATTERS FOR FRYING CHICKEN

(For one 2½- to 3-pound chicken)

1.   Combine 8 to 10 tablespoons of flour, 1 teaspoon of salt, and ¼ teaspoon of pepper. Either roll the pieces in this or put the flour mixture and the chicken in a paper bag, close tightly, and shake.

2.   Add 1½ teaspoons of paprika to the above and follow the same directions.

3.   Beat 1 egg till slightly foamy. Add ¼ cup of milk and mix. Roll the pieces of chicken in seasoned flour as above, dip them in the egg mixture, and then roll them in about 1 cup of fine bread or cracker crumbs.

4.   Combine 5 tablespoons of corn meal, 5 tablespoons of flour, 1 teaspoon of salt, and ¼ teaspoon of pepper. Either roll the pieces in this or put the meal-and-flour mixture and chicken in a paper bag and shake.

5.   Make a batter: Combine 1 cup of flour, 1 teaspoon of baking powder, and ¼ teaspoon of salt. Beat 1 egg till foamy and add to it ¾ cup of milk. Stir the liquid into the dry ingredients, and dip the pieces of chicken in this.

To roast: A whole fryer can be roasted in the same manner as a regular roaster or capon (see below) but, because it is still a young tender bird, I like to roast a fryer in a hotter (400°) oven for a shorter period of time. Also I like to cook a fryer unstuffed, saving the older birds to be stuffed.

Keep the chicken at room temperature for about an hour before you intend to roast it. Wipe the exterior with a slightly damp cloth. When the skin is dry, cover it completely with a film of softened, unsalted butter. Truss the bird so that the wings and legs are tied close to the body. Salt the cavity liberally and toss in a sprig of parsley (you can also sprinkle the cavity with a little dried thyme or tarragon; or, put in it a really big branch of fresh tarragon). Sew or skewer the opening. Tie a large flat piece of salt pork over the breast; or cover the breast with a cloth that has been saturated with melted butter; or cover it with a rectangle of aluminum foil. (Remove the fat or covering for the last 20 minutes of the cooking period.)

Place the chicken on a rack in an open roasting pan and put it in a preheated 400° oven. Cooking time should be from 1 to 1½ hours. Test a leg for doneness—no pink juice should run from a puncture and you should be able to move the leg in its socket. It is very important to baste the chicken often—every 10 to 15 minutes. You may have to add a little extra butter at first for the basting. Salt the skin two or three times during the cooking after basting.

Roasters (or chickens). Chickens of either sex whose ages range from 5 to 9 months. They weigh over 3½ pounds and they are tender, mature, and nicely plump. Although the obvious destiny of such birds is to be roasted, they can be braised.

To roast: Have the chicken at room temperature, wipe it with a slightly damp cloth. Sprinkle the cavity liberally with salt and loosely fill it with stuffing (see Recipe Index). Sew or skewer the opening, and sew or skewer the neck flap to the wing tips, which have been turned back under the bird. Truss by tying the legs tightly to the tail. Rub the entire exterior with soft unsalted butter and cover the breast with salt pork, or with a cloth saturated with melted butter, or with aluminum foil, as was described above for roasting a fryer. Remove the covering in this case for the last 30 minutes of the cooking time.

Place the chicken on a rack in an open roasting pan and put it in a preheated 325° oven. Cooking time for a small chicken will be about 45 minutes per pound, and for a larger bird, 30 minutes per pound. Baste occasionally and salt 2 or 3 times during the cooking, after basting. The chicken will be done when no pink juice runs from the leg and when the leg can be moved in its socket.

To braise: A whole braised chicken is lovely to look at, but to cook it properly you must truss it tightly. If you want to forego this procedure, cut the bird into serving pieces but cook it as you would the whole bird.

A whole braised chicken may be stuffed (see Index for Grandmother's Chicken); close the openings as tightly as possible. Truss the bird so that the legs and wings are tied tightly against the body. The idea is to make the chicken as compact as possible so that it can be easily and thoroughly browned.

Melt 4 tablespoons of butter in a Dutch oven or a large casserole that has a tight cover. Thoroughly brown the chicken on all sides—whole or in pieces—in the butter over brisk heat. To the pot then add cut up vegetables (carrot, onion, celery) that have been lightly sautéed in butter, and add seasonings and about ½ cup of liquid—water, stock, or a dry wine. Cover the pot and continue cooking over low heat on the top of the stove or in a 325° oven for 1 to 1½ hours.

Capons. Male chickens that have been castrated when 6 to 8 weeks of age. Capons generally weigh over 6 pounds when they come to market and are usually between 7 to 10 months of age. Despite their age, they have soft tender flesh; they also are "well padded." Because of their size, capons are the best choice for roasting if you have a good number of people to serve. Roast

as you would a roaster, counting on a little less cooking time—
from 22 to 30 minutes per pound, the longer time for the
smaller capon.

You may also braise a capon as you would a roaster.

Fowls or Hens. A female chicken becomes a fowl or a hen when
she has reached the age of one year or over. Fowls generally
weigh anywhere from 3 to 8 pounds. Their meat is not as
tender as that of a younger bird but it has a nice full flavor.
Long slow cooking—braising, stewing, fricasseeing, or poaching
—makes them delicious. They are often referred to as stewing
hens at the market.

To cook: Braise a fowl as you would a roaster or capon. The
cooking time should be lengthened to 2 hours or more. Consequently more liquid should be added to the pot; start with 1
cup, and do not let it cook away.

To stew a hen you need a pot large enough to hold about
3 cups of water or stock, various sliced vegetables, and the hen,
which has been cut into serving pieces. Brown the chicken in
hot butter first, if you like, or simply pour the boiling water
over it. Keep the water boiling while you add vegetables and
other flavorings, then cover the pot and reduce the heat to a
simmer. After an hour's cooking time add salt—½ teaspoon per
pound. The chicken should be tender after 2 hours or more
cooking time. Use some of the stock for gravy or a sauce. The
stewed meat can also be cut up and used in casseroles, salads, etc.

When you fricassee a hen (or chicken) you simply stew it without browning the pieces first. A fricassee calls for a special sauce
(and there are variations, of course) to be made from the liquid
in which the bird has been cooked.

You should poach a hen whose age indicates that it would be

tough braised for only 2 hours in a small amount of liquid. In other words, a "dowager" hen requires enough boiling water to cover and a simmering time of maybe 3 to 4 hours. You may stuff and truss this hen as you would for braising. Also add the same flavorings and vegetables to the water.

Cocks, Roosters, or Stags. These birds are males that have passed their first birthday. They are quite tough; their meat is dark and strong in flavor. I simply mention them in passing.

Chicken Livers. The chicken has one delicious internal organ—its liver. The liver is generally quite small and you need a number of them for one serving, but you can usually buy them by the pound.

Chicken Recipes

See Chapter 8 for a number of sauces that are good with chicken.

BROILED DEVILED CHICKEN

(For 4)

2 large or 4 small broilers
⅓ cup butter, melted
Salt
1 tablespoon prepared mustard thinned with 1 teaspoon water
Cayenne pepper
1 cup dry bread crumbs
1 cup Devil Sauce (see Index)
Lemon wedges

Prepare the chickens for broiling (see p. 282). Thoroughly coat each piece with melted butter and sprinkle them with salt. Preheat the broiler to 375° and cook the chickens 3½ to 4 inches from the heat for 15 minutes per side. When the chickens have broiled for 30 minutes, remove them from the broiler, spread them on the skin sides with the thinned mustard to which a sprinkle of cayenne has been added. Roll the skin sides in the bread crumbs, pressing the crumbs into the skin. Pour the remaining butter over the chickens, return them to the broiler, skin side up, and cook to a golden brown. Serve with Devil Sauce and lemon wedges.

MARINATED BROILERS
(For 4)

- 2 large or 4 small broilers
- 1 cup olive oil
- ½ cup dry white wine
- 1 clove garlic, minced
- 3 green onions, minced
- ½ teaspoon coarsely ground pepper
- 1 teaspoon dried chervil
- 2 tablespoons chopped parsley

Prepare the chickens for broiling (see p. 282). Combine all other ingredients in a deep platter large enough to accommodate the chickens. Marinate for at least 1 hour, turning each piece so that both sides come in contact with the marinade. Preheat the broiler to 375° and cook the chickens 3½ to 4 inches from the heat. Allow 15 to 20 minutes per side, basting often with the marinade.

CHICKEN MARSEILLAISE
(For 4)

- 1 large or 2 small fryers, cut into serving pieces
- 2 tablespoons olive oil
- 2½ cloves garlic
- Salt and pepper
- 2 tablespoons butter
- 1 large or 2 small green peppers, cut into strips
- 3 fresh tomatoes, peeled, seeded, and chopped
- ¼ cup chicken stock
- 2 tablespoons dry white wine
- 1 tablespoon chopped parsley

Heat the olive oil in a large skillet and sauté in it for a minute one clove of the garlic which has first been cut into strips. Salt and pepper the chicken pieces and add them to the oil. Allow the pieces to brown, then reduce the heat and cover the pan.

In another skillet melt the butter, and in it sauté the green-pepper strips and another clove of garlic, chopped, for 10 minutes. Add the tomatoes and cook for another 10 minutes.

When the chicken has cooked for 30 minutes, pour off any excess oil in the pan, and add the green-pepper-tomato mixture, the stock, and the wine to the chicken. Cook slowly, uncovered, for 10 to 15 minutes. Correct the seasoning with salt and pepper. Serve on a platter, garnished with chopped parsley and the remaining ½ clove of garlic that has been very finely minced.

HUNTER'S CHICKEN
(For 4)

1 large or 2 small fryers, cut into serving pieces
Salt and pepper
3 tablespoons butter, or half butter and half olive oil
¼ lb. fresh mushrooms, sliced
1 tablespoon minced green onion
1 tablespoon flour
¼ cup chicken stock
¼ cup dry white wine
1 tablespoon tomato paste
Pinch each dried chervil and tarragon
Sprig parsley, chopped
1 teaspoon brandy (optional)

Salt and pepper the chicken pieces. Melt the butter in a skillet, brown the chicken in it, reduce the heat, and continue cooking with the pan covered. At the end of 30 minutes, add the mush-rooms and cook for another 10 to 15 minutes with the pan un-covered. Remove the chicken to a hot platter. Add the onion to the mushrooms left in the skillet and sauté for 1 to 2 minutes. Mix in the flour and slowly stir in the stock and wine. Let this mixture simmer and thicken for about 5 minutes, stirring con-stantly. Add the tomato paste, chervil, tarragon, and brandy. Mix thoroughly, correct the seasoning with salt and pepper, and pour the sauce over the chicken. Garnish with chopped parsley.

CHICKEN PAPRIKA

(For 4)

1 large or 2 small fryers, cut into serving pieces
Salt
2 tablespoons Hungarian paprika
Flour
3 tablespoons butter
1 large onion, minced
½ cup chicken stock
½ cup sour cream

Season the chicken pieces with salt and the paprika, and dredge them with flour. Melt the butter in a large skillet and sauté the onion in it until transparent. Add the chicken pieces and brown them on all sides. Cover the skillet and simmer for 30 minutes, then remove the cover and simmer for another 15 minutes or until the chicken is tender. Remove the chicken to a hot platter. Into the butter remaining in the skillet stir 1 tablespoon of flour and any remaining paprika. Slowly add the stock, and cook this until it thickens, stirring constantly. Stir in the sour cream and heat the sauce but do not allow it to boil. Serve with the sauce poured over the chicken.

ROAST CHICKEN WITH TARRAGON

(For 4)

1 large fryer, whole, prepared for roasting
4 tablespoons unsalted butter, in all
The chicken's liver
¼ cup dry white wine
Salt
1 tablespoon chopped parsley
½ teaspoon dried tarragon
1 clove garlic

Melt 2 tablespoons of the butter in a saucepan, and in it lightly sauté the chicken liver until it is golden brown. Add the wine and allow it to boil gently for 3 to 4 minutes. Salt the cavity of the chicken well and sprinkle it with the tarragon and parsley. Add the garlic and pour in the liver-wine mixture. Skewer or sew the openings, and truss the bird so that the legs and wings are as close to the body as possible. Rub the entire outside of the chicken with the remaining 2 tablespoons of butter which has been softened to room temperature.

Place the chicken on a rack, cover the breast with a piece of salt pork or a cloth saturated with butter, and roast in a 400° oven. Cooking time should be 1 to 1½ hours. Twenty minutes before the bird is done, remove the breast covering and sprinkle the chicken with a good amount of salt (do not re-cover the breast). During the entire cooking period the chicken should be basted every 10 to 15 minutes with the drippings in the pan.

GRANDMOTHER'S CHICKEN

(For 4 or 6)

1 roaster, whole, dressed, ready to cook
2 tablespoons butter
6 ozs. salt pork, cut into ½-inch cubes
10 small white onions
3 to 4 potatoes, peeled and cut into small cubes

Stuffing:

2 tablespoons butter
1 onion, minced
¼ lb. ground pork (preferably from Boston butt)
1 chicken liver, chopped
2 tablespoons chopped parsley
2 cups bread crumbs, about
1 teaspoon salt
¼ teaspoon dried thyme
¼ teaspoon pepper

Stuffing: Melt the butter in a skillet and in it sauté the onion until it is transparent. Mix in the ground pork, chicken liver, parsley, bread crumbs, and seasonings. Cook over medium heat for 5 minutes, stirring constantly.

Stuff the roaster and truss well. In a casserole large enough to accommodate both the chicken and the potatoes melt the 2 tablespoons of butter and add the salt pork. Put in the chicken and brown it on all sides over medium heat, basting often; this should take about 30 minutes. Then add the onions and allow them to color. Add the potato cubes. Cover the casserole tightly and continue cooking over low heat, or in a 325° oven, for 1 to

1½ hours or until the chicken is tender. One half hour before the chicken is done, taste and add a little salt if necessary. Serve in the casserole.

VAUCLUSE CHICKEN

(For 4 or 6)

1 roaster, whole, dressed, ready to cook
Salt and pepper
2 ozs. ground pork (preferably from Boston butt)
2 tablespoons olive oil
1 onion, finely minced
½ cup dry white wine
3 to 4 tomatoes, peeled, seeded, and minced
Sprig parsley, chopped
1 clove garlic, sliced
24 black pitted olives

Season the cavity of the roaster well with salt and pepper. Truss the bird tightly and place it in a casserole with the ground pork and olive oil. Brown quickly on all sides over high heat. When the chicken is brown, add the onion and allow it to color. Pour in the wine, add the tomatoes, parsley, and garlic. Cover the casserole tightly and cook over low heat, or in a 325° oven, for 1 to 1½ hours. When the chicken is almost done, add the olives and correct the seasoning with salt and pepper. Serve from the casserole.

SUPREME CHICKEN

(For 4 or 6)

1 fowl, whole, dressed, ready to cook
1 onion, stuck with a clove
1 large carrot
1 stalk celery
1 bay leaf
1/4 teaspoon dried thyme
Sprig parsley
Boiling water
Salt (1/2 teaspoon per pound of chicken)
4 tablespoons butter, in all
1/2 lb. fresh mushrooms, sliced
2 tablespoons flour
1/2 cup heavy cream

Truss the fowl well, so that the wings and legs are as close to the body as possible. Place it in a deep kettle and add the onion, carrot, celery, bay leaf, thyme, and parsley. Pour boiling water into the kettle until the fowl is just submerged. Cover the kettle tightly, and cook over the lowest possible heat for 3 to 4 hours, or until the chicken is tender. After the first hour of cooking, add the salt.

When the chicken is done, pour off 2 cups of the broth and strain it through a sieve. Keep the chicken warm in the remaining liquid. Sauté the mushrooms in 2 tablespoons of the butter. In another pan, melt the remaining butter, and stir in the flour. Slowly add the strained broth, blend well, and bring to a vigorous boil to reduce the volume by one half. Then lower the heat, add the cream, and stir until the sauce coats the spoon. Add the mushrooms and the butter in which they were sautéed. Serve the chicken on a hot platter with the sauce poured over it.

FRIED HEN

(For 4 or 6)

1 hen, dressed, ready to cook
Boiling water
1 onion stuck with a clove
1 large carrot
1 stalk celery
1 bay leaf
¼ teaspoon dried thyme
Sprig parsley
Salt (½ teaspoon per pound of chicken)
¼ cup olive oil
Juice 1 lemon
1 tablespoon chopped parsley
Fat for frying
Batter (see #5, p. 286)
1 cup Portuguese Sauce (see Index)

Place the hen in a deep kettle, add enough boiling water just to submerge it, and add the onion, carrot, celery, bay leaf, thyme, and parsley. Cover the kettle and gently simmer the chicken until tender (2 to 4 hours). Add the salt after the first hour of cooking. When the hen is done, let it cool in the broth, and then carefully remove the meat from the bones. Cut into pieces as uniform as possible—approximately 1-inch cubes. Place the pieces in a bowl, and add the olive oil, lemon juice, and parsley. Mix, allow to marinate for 1 hour, then drain the pieces well. Make the batter.

In a deep pan melt the fat to a depth of 1 inch. Dip the pieces of chicken in the batter and fry them quickly in the very hot fat until they are golden. Drain well. Serve the pieces on a hot platter, garnished with parsley or vegetables, and serve the Portuguese Sauce in a gravy boat.

STUFFING FOR CHICKEN

(Allow ½ to ¾ cup per pound)

¼ lb. butter
1 medium onion, finely chopped
½ cup finely chopped celery
The chicken's liver, chopped (optional)
3 cups dry bread crumbs *
½ teaspoon dried thyme, or ½ teaspoon each thyme and
   marjoram, or ¼ teaspoon sage
1 tablespoon chopped parsley
Salt and pepper

Sauté the onion, celery, and liver in the butter until the onion is transparent. Remove from the stove and thoroughly mix in the remaining ingredients. Salt and pepper to taste. Do not stuff the chicken until this mixture is thoroughly cool, and stuff the bird loosely.

* You may replace the bread crumbs with 1¼ cups of wild rice that has been rinsed, boiled for 20 minutes in 4 cups of salted water, and drained.

SKEWERED CHICKEN LIVERS
(For 4)

24 chicken livers
7 tablespoons butter, in all
1/3 lb. salt pork
24 fresh mushrooms
1 teaspoon chopped parsley
1/2 teaspoon lemon juice
1/4 teaspoon dry mustard

Heat 3 tablespoons of the butter in a skillet until it foams, and in it quickly sauté the livers until they are firm outside but not cooked through. Remove them from the pan. Cut the salt pork into 24 small cubes, and parboil these in a small amount of water for 5 minutes; drain well. In the butter in which the livers have cooked, lightly sauté the mushrooms. Place the livers, salt-pork cubes, and mushrooms on skewers, alternating six of each to a skewer. Brush each skewerful with the butter that remains in the skillet, and salt and pepper them. Broil under moderately high heat until well browned (about 5 minutes), turning often.

Serve on the skewers and spread with seasoned butter: Let the remaining 4 tablespoons of butter warm to room temperature, and blend into it the parsley, lemon juice, and mustard.

CHICKEN LIVERS WITH MUSHROOMS

(For 4)

1 lb. chicken livers
4 tablespoons butter
½ lb. fresh mushrooms, or 6-oz. can mushrooms
1 tablespoon finely chopped green pepper
1 tablespoon finely chopped parsley
1 tablespoon finely chopped onion
2 tablespoons flour
1 cup chicken stock
½ cup dry white wine
½ bay leaf
Pinch dried thyme
Dash nutmeg
Salt and pepper

Heat the butter in a skillet and brown the livers in it for about 5 to 6 minutes. Remove the livers to another pan and keep them warm. Sauté the mushrooms, green pepper, parsley, and onion in the same butter for 5 minutes. Stir in the flour, and slowly add the chicken stock and wine, stirring constantly. Add the bay leaf and thyme and simmer together for 5 to 6 minutes, or until the sauce is thickened. Remove the bay leaf, and add the nutmeg, and salt and pepper to taste. At the last minute reheat the livers in the sauce. Be sure they are heated through, but do not overcook. Serve with rice.

APPENDIX

BROILING TIMES AND TEMPERATURES *

BEEF

Cut and Thickness	Minutes per Side			
	Rare		Medium	
	At 350°	At high heat	At 350°	At high heat
Sirloin Steak				
1 inch	10	5-6	12	6-7
1½ inches	15	9-10	17	10-12
2 inches	20	17	22	18-20
Porterhouse				
1 inch	10	4-5	12	6-7
1½ inches	15	8-9	17	10-11
2 inches	20	13-14	22	17-18
Club Steak				
1 inch	7	4-5	10	6-7
1½ inches	12	8-9	15	10-11
2 inches	17	13-14	22	17-18
Filet Mignon				
1 inch	—	2-3	—	3-4
1½ inches	—	4-5	—	5-6
2 inches	—	5-6	—	7-8

For all steaks over 2 inches thick: Sear each side and then cook at 350° for 20 minutes per side; test both sides, cook longer if necessary.

LAMB CHOPS

Thickness	Min. per Side at 350°	Searing Method † Min. per Side after Searing
1 inch	6	4-5
1½ inches	9	6-7
2 inches	11	8-10

HAM SLICE

Thickness	Minutes per Side At 400°-450°	
⅓ inch	3-4	
½ inch	5-6	Cut broiling time in half
¾ inch	7-8	if ham is precooked
1 inch	10-12	

---

* For guidance on broiling frozen meats, see p. 47.
† Sear first at 500°, then cook at 350°.

Roasting Times and Temperatures *

Cut	Minutes per Pound (approximately)	Meat Thermometer Reading	Oven Temperature
BEEF			
Standing rump			
Standing rib			
rare	18-20	140°	
medium	22-25	160°	
well done	27-30	170°	
Rolled rump			
Rolled rib			325°
rare	32	140°	
medium	38	160°	
well done	48	170°	
Filet (whole)			
rare	Entire time never	140°	
medium	longer than 40 minutes	160°	

Cut	Minutes per Pound (approximately)	Meat Thermometer Reading	Oven Temperature
VEAL			
Leg	25-30		
Rump			
Sirloin	30-35		
Loin		170°	325°
Standing rib			
Rolled rib	40-45		
Shoulder (blade or arm)	25		
Stuffed shoulder	40-45		
Breast (stuffed or rolled)			

* For the searing and all-day methods, see pp. 55-56. Remember that, as a rule, small roasts require more time per pound than large roasts and boned roasts require more time than roasts with bones. See p. 47 for guidance on roasting frozen meats.

Cut	Minutes per Pound (approximately)	Meat Thermometer Reading	Oven Temperature
LAMB			
Leg			
Loin			
rare	20	160°-165°	
medium	25-30	175°	
well done	30-35	180°	
Boneless sirloin			
Rolled loin			
rare	30	160°-165°	
medium	35-40	175°	
well done	40-45	180°	
Rib			
Crown			
rare		160°-165°	300°-325°
medium	10-15 *	175°	
well done		180°	
Square-cut shoulder			
medium		175°	
well done	30-35 *	180°	
Cushion shoulder			
medium		175°	
well done	35-40 *	180°	
Rolled shoulder			
medium		175°	
well done	40-45 *	180°	
Rolled breast	35	175°-180°	

* For these cuts, thermometer reading is best indication of whether meat is rare, medium, or well done.

Cut	Minutes per Pound (approximately)	Meat Thermometer Reading	Oven Temperature
FRESH PORK			
Leg	30-45		
Tenderloin	35		
Sirloin			
Blade loin	45-50		
Boston butt			
Boneless sirloin	50		
Loin	35-40	185°	350°
Crown			
Picnic shoulder			
with bones	30-35		
rolled	40-45		
cushion	35-40		
Spareribs	30-35		
CURED PORK			
Ham (uncooked, mild-cure)			
large	15-18		
medium	18-22	165°	300°
small	22-25		
Ham (precooked, mild-cure)	15-20	130°	325°
Ham (country-cured, after simmering)			
Total time:	45-60	130°	350°
Canadian-style bacon (unsliced)	25	160°	350°
Smoked shoulder butt	35-40	170°	300°
Smoked picnic shoulder	35	170°	300°
CHICKEN			
Whole fryer	12-15	—	400°
Roaster	30-45	—	325°
Capon	22-30	—	325°

Bibliography

Beck, S., Bertholle, L., and Child, J., *Mastering the Art of French Cooking*. New York, Alfred A. Knopf, Inc., 1961.

Beef: facts for consumer education, No. AIB 84. U.S. Department of Agriculture, 1952.

Better Homes & Gardens Meat Cook Book. Des Moines, Meredith Publishing Co., 1960.

Bull, Sleeter, *Meat for the Table*. New York, McGraw-Hill Book Co., Inc., 1951.

David, Elizabeth, *French Provincial Cooking*. New York, Harper & Row, Publishers, 1962.

Flammarion, Ernest, ed., *The Art of French Cooking*. New York, Simon & Schuster, Inc., 1958.

Meat Manual, 5th ed. Chicago, National Live Stock and Meat Board, 1952.

Meat Reference Book. Chicago, American Meat Institute, 1960.

Montagné, Prosper, *Larousse Gastronomique: The Encyclopedia of Food, Wine, and Cookery*. New York: Crown Publishers, Inc., 1961.

Pork: facts for consumer education, No. AIB 109. U.S. Department of Agriculture, 1954.

Rombauer, Irma S., and Becker, Marion R., *The Joy of Cooking*. Indianapolis, The Bobbs-Merrill Co., 1953.

Ten Lessons on Meat for Use in Schools, 6th ed. Chicago, National Live Stock and Meat Board, 1943.

Ziegler, P. Thomas, *The Meat We Eat,* 4th ed. Danville, Ill., The Interstate Printers and Publishers, 1954.

INDEX

Page numbers in **boldface** refer to drawings, charts, or photographs.
Recipes are *italicized*.